PERFORMANCE-BASED STANDARDS FOR ADULT PROBATION AND PAROLE FIELD SERVICES,

4th Edition

American Correctional Association
In cooperation with the
Commission on Accreditation for Corrections

2010

Mission of the American Correctional Association
The American Correctional Association provides a professional organization for all individuals and groups, both public and private, that share a common goal of improving the justice system.

Information on accreditation may be obtained from:
American Correctional Association, Standards and Accreditation Department, 206 N. Washington Street, Suite 200, Alexandria, VA 22314   (800) 222-5646

American Correctional Association Staff
Harold W. Clarke, President
James A. Gondles, Jr., CAE, Executive Director
Gabriella M. Klatt, Director, Communications and Publications
Alice Heiserman, Manager of Publications and Research
Jeannelle Ferreira, Associate Editor
Xavaire Bolton, Graphics and Production Associate
Cover designed by Leigh Ann Bright, Graphics and Production Associate

Printed in the United States of America by Gasch Printing, Odenton, MD

Cover Credits: Lower left: Field Operations Division, Georgia State Board of Pardons and Paroles; Lower right: Kentucky Division of Probation and Parole

This publication may be ordered from:
American Correctional Association
(800) 222-5646 ext. 0129

For information on publications and videos available from ACA, visit our Web site: www.aca.org/store.

ISBN: 978-1-56991-323-9

Contents

Standards Manuals Published by the American Correctional Association

2010 Standards Supplement

Core Jail Standards

Standards for the Administration of Correctional Agencies

Performance-Based Standards for Adult Community Residential Services

Standards for Adult Correctional Boot Camp Programs

Standards for Adult Correctional Institutions

Standards for Adult Correctional Institutions (Spanish Version)

Performance-Based Standards for Adult Local Detention Facilities

Standards for Adult Parole Authorities

Performance-Based Standards for Adult Probation and Parole Field Services

Performance-Based Standards for Correctional Health Care for Adult Correctional Institutions

Performance-Based Standards for Correctional Industries

Performance-Based Standards for Therapeutic Communities

Standards for Correctional Training Academies

Standards for Electronic Monitoring Programs

Standards for Juvenile Community Residential Facilities

Standards for Juvenile Correctional Boot Camp Programs

Performance-Based Standards for Juvenile Correctional Facilities

Standards for Juvenile Day Treatment Programs

Standards for Juvenile Detention Facilities

Standards for Juvenile Probation and Aftercare Services

Standards for Small Juvenile Detention Facilities

These publications may be ordered from ACA:

www.aca.org or (800) 222-5646 ext. 0129

Foreword

According to the Bureau of Justice Statistics, at the end of 2008 there were 5.1 million people under community correctional supervision. The number of U.S. parolees has jumped 19 percent since 2006, and probation is the fastest-growing segment in the correctional field.

This edition of *Performance-Based Standards for Adult Probation and Parole Field Services* is the result of two years' diligent review and field testing by the Standards Committee and the Commission on Accreditation for Corrections. Updated after twelve years to reflect the changing landscape of community corrections, the manual incorporates feedback from practitioners in the field and has been formatted in the performance-based model.

With the closure of many prisons and jails and the reduction in populations, a revised set of standards for probation and parole is extremely relevant. Our hope is that this manual will help community corrections professionals do their work with greater efficiency, introduce new, more effective practices, and build safer neighborhoods through reduced recidivism. Many thanks to the individuals and organizations who provided recommendations for revision and participated in the field testing.

James A. Gondles, Jr., CAE
Executive Director
American Correctional Association

Commission on Accreditation for Corrections

AMERICAN CORRECTIONAL ASSOCIATION 2008-2010

Officers

Harold W. Clarke, Massachusetts, President
Patricia L. Caruso, Michigan, Vice President
Daron Hall, Tennessee, President-Elect
Christopher Epps, Mississippi, Treasurer
Gary Maynard, Maryland, Immediate Past President
Mark H. Saunders, Ohio, Board of Governor's Representative
Ana T. Aguirre, Texas, Board of Governor's Representative
James A. Gondles, Jr., CAE, Executive Director

Board of Governors

Ekpe D. Ekpe, New York
Joyce Fogg, Virginia
David A. Gaspar, Arizona
Jeanna Gomez, Texas
Robert L. Guy, North Carolina
Gail M. Heller, Ohio
Lawrence E. Hicks, Oklahoma
Artis R. Hobbs, Arkansas
Mary V. Leftridge Byrd, Georgia
George Little, Tennessee
Mary L. Livers, Louisiana
Walter A. McFarlane, Virginia
David M. Parrish, Florida
Kathy Pittman, Mississippi
Robert Rosenbloom, Georgia
Mark H. Saunders, Ohio
Shannon D. Teague, Ohio
David L. Thomas, Florida

Committee on Standards

Harley Lappin, Washington, D.C., Chair
Lannette Linthicum, Texas, Vice Chair
Kathleen Bachmeier, North Dakota
Jeffrey A. Beard, Pennsylvania
Ronald Budzinski, Illinois
Daniel Craig, Iowa
Brian Fischer, New York
Steve Gibson, Montana
Stanley Glanz, Oklahoma
David Haasenritter, Virginia
Justin Jones, Oklahoma
James LeBlanc, Louisiana
Mary Livers, Louisiana
Denise Robinson, Ohio
Marilyn Rogan, Nevada
Paula Smith, North Carolina
William Thompson, Texas
Marge Webster, New Hampshire

Executive Office

James A. Gondles, Jr., CAE, Executive Director
Jeffrey Washington, Deputy Executive Director
Jennifer Bechtel, Director, Grants and Administration
India Vargas, Senior Administrative Assistant

Standards and Accreditation Staff

Kathy Black-Dennis, Director
Pam Eckler, Accreditation Specialist
Terri Jackson, Accreditation Specialist
Christina Randolph, Office Manager
Irawaty Bakker, Administrative Assistant
Terry Carter, Administrative Assistant
Nadine Lee, Administrative Assistant

Introduction to Accreditation

The American Correctional Association (ACA) and the Commission on Accreditation for Corrections (CAC) are private, nonprofit organizations that administer the only national accreditation program for all components of adult and juvenile corrections. Their purpose is to promote improvement in the management of correctional agencies through the administration of a voluntary accreditation program and the ongoing development and revision of relevant, useful standards.

Accreditation, a process that began in 1978, involves a large number of detention facilities and approximately 80 percent of all state departments of corrections, Puerto Rico, the military, and youth services as active participants. Also included are programs and facilities operated by the Federal Bureau of Prisons, the U.S. Parole Commission, and the District of Columbia. For these agencies, the accreditation program offers the opportunity to evaluate their operations against national standards, remedy deficiencies, and upgrade the quality of correctional programs and services. The recognized benefits from such a process include improved management, a defense against lawsuits through documentation and the demonstration of a "good faith" effort to improve conditions of confinement, increased accountability and enhanced public credibility for administrative and line staff, a safer and more humane environment for personnel and offenders, and the establishment of measurable criteria for upgrading programs, personnel, and the physical plant on a continuing basis.

The timelines, requirements, and outcomes of the accreditation process are the same for a state or federal prison, training school, local detention facility, private halfway house or group home, probation and parole field service agency, or paroling authority. All programs and facilities sign a contract, pay an accreditation fee, conduct a self-evaluation, and have a standards compliance audit by trained ACA auditors before an accreditation decision is made by the Commission on Accreditation for Corrections. Once accredited, all programs and facilities submit annual certification statements to ACA. Also, at ACA's expense and discretion, a monitoring visit may be conducted during the initial three-year accreditation period to ensure continued compliance with the appropriate standards.

Participation in the Accreditation Process

Invitations to participate in the accreditation process have been extended to all adult and juvenile agencies for which standards have been developed and published. Participating agencies include public and private agencies; federal, state, and local agencies; and United States and Canadian correctional agencies.

Accreditation activities are initiated voluntarily by correctional administrators. When an agency chooses to pursue accreditation, ACA staff will provide the agency with appropriate information and application materials. These include a contract, the applicable manual of standards, a policy and procedure manual, and an organization summary.

Eligibility Criteria

To be eligible for accreditation, an agency must be a part of a governmental or private entity or conform to the applicable federal, state, or local laws and regulations regarding corporate existence. The agency must: (1) hold under confinement pretrial or presentenced adults or juveniles who are being held pending a hearing for unlawful activity; or (2) hold under confinement sentenced adult offenders convicted of criminal activity or juveniles adjudicated to confinement; or (3) supervise in the community sentenced adult or adjudicated juvenile offenders, including juveniles placed in residential settings; and (4) have a single administrative officer responsible for agency operations. It is this administrative officer who makes formal application for admission for accreditation.

It is ACA's policy that nonadjudicated juveniles should be served outside the juvenile correctional system. Training schools housing status offenders must remove them before the facility can be awarded accreditation. Detention facilities may house status offenders who have violated valid court orders by continued perpetration of status offenses. In such instances, the following conditions would apply: status offenders are separated by sight and sound from delinquent offenders; facility staff demonstrate attempts to mandate removal of all status offenders from detention centers; and special programs are developed for status offenders.

ACA does not prohibit community programs that house adjudicated juveniles with status offenders in nonsecure settings from participation in accreditation. However, ACA actively supports and requires exclusion of status offenders from the criminal and juvenile justice systems. Residential facilities and institutional programs that house adults and juveniles separated by sight and sound may become accredited. Individual cases may stipulate removal of juveniles before receiving an accreditation award.

Preaccreditation Assessment

Prior to signing an accreditation contract, an agency may request a preaccreditation assessment. The assessment requires an ACA auditor to visit the agency. The auditor will assess strengths and areas for improvement, measure readiness for application for accreditation, and identify steps required to achieve accreditation. A confidential, written report is provided to the agency to assist in making the decision to apply for accreditation.

Applicant Status

When the agency enters into the accreditation process, the administrator requests an information package from ACA. To confirm eligibility, determine appropriate fees, and schedule accreditation activities, the agency provides ACA with relevant narrative information through the organization summary. Applicant Status begins when both the completed organization summary, which provides a written description of the facility/program and the signed contract are returned to ACA. The Association will notify the agency of its acceptance into the accreditation process within fifteen days of the receipt of the necessary application materials. ACA will then assign a regional administrator from the Standards and Accreditation Department as a permanent liaison to the agency. The agency will appoint an accreditation manager, who will be responsible for organizing and supervising agency resources and activities to achieve accreditation.

As defined in the contract, the fees for the accreditation period cover all services normally provided to an agency by ACA staff, auditors, and the Commission. The fees are determined during the application period and are included in the contract signed by the agency and ACA.

Correspondent Status

When the application is accepted, the agency enters into Correspondent Status. During this time, the agency conducts a self-assessment of its operations and completes a self-evaluation report, which specifies the agency's level of standards compliance. (Self-evaluation reports are optional for facilities signing a reaccreditation contract.)

At the agency's request and expense, an on-site accreditation orientation for staff and/or a field consultation may be scheduled. The object of the orientation is to prepare agency staff to complete the requirements of accreditation, including an understanding of self-evaluation activities, compilation of documentation, audit procedures, and standards interpretation. A field auditor provides information on accreditation policy and procedure, standards interpretations, and/or documentation requirements. Agency familiarity with standards and accreditation is the key factor in determining the need for these services.

The self-evaluation report includes the organizational summary, a compliance tally, preliminary requests for waivers or plans of action, and a completed standards compliance checklist for each standard in the applicable manual.

Applicable Standards

The standards used for accreditation address services, programs, and operations essential to good correctional management, including administrative, staff, and fiscal controls, staff training and development, physical plant, safety and emergency procedures, sanitation, food service, rules and discipline, and a variety of subjects that comprise good correctional practice. These standards are under continual revision to reflect changing practice, current case law, new knowledge, and agency experience with their application. These changes are published by ACA in the *Standards Supplement*.

ACA policy addresses the impact of the standards revisions on agencies involved in accreditation. Agencies signing contracts after the date that a *Standards Supplement* is published are held accountable for all standards changes in that supplement. Agencies are not held accountable for changes made after the contract is signed. The agencies may choose to apply new changes to the standards that have been issued following the program's entry into accreditation. Agencies must notify ACA of their decision before conducting the standards compliance audit.

For accreditation purposes, any new architectural design, building, and/or renovation of the institution must be in accordance with the current standards manual at the time of the design, building, and/or renovation. In such cases, different standards would be applied to separate parts of the institution, respective to these changes in the physical plant.

Standards Compliance Checklist

In completing a standards compliance checklist, the agency checks compliance, noncompliance, or not applicable for each standard. Checking compliance signifies complete compliance with the content of the standard at all times and that the agency has documentation (primarily written) available to support compliance. A finding of noncompliance indicates that all or part of the requirements stated in the standard have not been met. A not applicable response means that the standard/expected practice is clearly not relevant to the agency/facility being audited. A written statement supporting nonapplicability of the standard/expected practice is required.

At this time, the agency may request a waiver for one or more standards, provided that overall agency programming compensates for the lack of compliance. The waiver request must be accompanied by a clear explanation of the compensating conditions. The agency applies for a waiver only when the totality of conditions safeguard the life, health, and safety of offenders and staff. Waivers are not granted for standards/expected practices designated as mandatory and do not change the conclusion of noncompliance or the agency's compliance tally. When a waiver is requested during the self-evaluation phase, ACA staff renders a preliminary judgment. A final decision can be made only by the Board of Commissioners during the accreditation hearing. Most waivers granted are for physical plant standards.

The Association requires that a self-evaluation report be completed by each applicant for accreditation. It is recommended that agencies entering into the accreditation process for the first time submit a written statement to ACA concerning their status at the completion of the evaluation. Information contained in this statement should include the percentage of compliance with mandatory and nonmandatory standards; a list of not applicable standards/expected practices; and a list of noncompliant standards and their deficiencies. Within sixty days of receipt of this statement, ACA staff will provide the agency administrator with a written response containing, where appropriate, comments on materials or information submitted to the Association. The letter also provides notice to the agency of its acceptance to Candidate Status.

The compilation of written documentation requires the most time and effort during Correspondent Status. A separate documentation file, which documents compliance, is prepared for each standard.

To request an audit, an agency must comply with 100 percent of the standards and expected practices designated as mandatory and 90 percent of the nonmandatory standards/expected practices.

Candidate Status

The agency enters into Candidate Status with ACA's acceptance of the self-evaluation report or agency certification of its completion. Candidate Status continues until the agency meets the required level of compliance, has been audited by a visiting committee composed of ACA auditors, and has been awarded or denied a three-year accreditation by the Board of Commissioners. Candidate Status lasts up to twelve months.

The agency requests a standards compliance audit when the facility administrator believes the agency or facility has met or exceeded the compliance levels required for accreditation (100 percent mandatory, 90 percent nonmandatory).

Standards Compliance Audit

The agency's request for an audit is made six to eight weeks before the desired audit dates. The purpose of the audit is to have the visiting committee measure the agency's operation against the standards based on the documentation provided by the agency. A visiting committee completes the audit and prepares a visiting committee report for submission to the Commission. ACA designates a visiting committee chair to organize and supervise the committee's activities.

Prior to arrival at the audit site, each member of the visiting committee reviews the agency's descriptive narrative and any additional information that ACA may have provided, including pending litigation and court orders submitted by the agency and any inmate correspondence. The visiting committee chair makes audit assignments to each auditor. For example, one auditor may audit the administrative, fiscal, and personnel standards/expected practices, while another audits standards/expected practices for physical plant, sanitation, and security. Upon arrival, the visiting committee meets with the administrator, accreditation manager, and other appropriate staff to discuss the scope of the audit and the schedule of activities. This exchange of information provides for the development of an audit schedule that ensures the least amount of disruption to routine agency operation.

The exact amount of time required to complete the audit depends on agency size, number of applicable standards/expected practices, additional facilities to be audited, and accessibility and organization of documentation. To hasten the audit, all documentation should be clearly referenced and located where the visiting committee is to work.

The accreditation manager's responsibilities include compiling and making accessible to all visiting committee members the standards compliance documentation and release-of-information forms for personnel and offender records. Also, staff should be notified beforehand to ensure that they are available to discuss specific issues or conduct tours of the facility for the visiting committee.

During the audit, the members of the visiting committee tour the facility, review documentation prepared for each standard/expected practice, and interview staff and offenders to make compliance decisions. The visiting committee reports its findings on the same standards-compliance checklist used by the agency in preparing its self-evaluation report. All members of the visiting committee review all mandatory standards/expected practices, all areas of noncompliance and nonapplicability, with decisions made collectively. (Final decisions on waivers can be approved only by the Commission at the time of the agency's accreditation hearing.)

Interviewing staff and offenders is an integral part of the audit. In addition to speaking with those who request an interview with the team, the members of the visiting committee select other individuals to interview and with whom to discuss issues. Interviews are voluntary and occur randomly throughout the audit, and those interviewed are ensured that their discussions are confidential.

In addition to auditing standards/expected practices documentation, auditors will evaluate the quality of life or conditions of confinement. An acceptable quality of life is necessary for an agency to be eligible for accreditation. Factors that the visiting committee consider include: the adequacy and quality of programs, activities, and services available to offenders and their involvement; occurrences of disturbances, serious incidents, assaults, or violence, including their frequency and methods of dealing with them to ensure the safety of staff and offenders or juveniles; and overall physical conditions, including conditions of confinement, program space, and institutional maintenance related to sanitation, health, and safety.

At the conclusion of the audit, the visiting committee again meets with the administrator, the accreditation manager, and any others selected by the administrator to discuss the results of the audit. During this exit interview, the visiting committee reports the compliance tally and all findings of noncompliance and nonapplicability, as well as preliminary decisions on waivers, stating the reasons for each decision.

The chair of the visiting committee then prepares and submits a copy of the visiting committee report to ACA staff within ten days of the completion of the audit. ACA staff review the report for completeness, enters the data, and within fifteen days of the audit's completion, it is submitted to the agency administrator and other members of the visiting committee for concurrence. Upon receipt of the visiting committee report, the agency has seven days to submit its written response to the report to ACA staff and all members of the visiting committee.

The Accreditation Hearing

The Commission on Accreditation for Corrections is responsible for rendering accreditation decisions and is divided into accreditation panels authorized to render such decisions. Panels meet separately, or with a full board meeting, and are composed of three-to-five commissioners.

The agency is invited to have representation at the accreditation hearing. Unless circumstances dictate otherwise, a member of the visiting committee is not present; however, an ACA staff member does participate. At the accreditation hearing, the agency representative provides information about the agency, speaks in support of its appeal and/or waiver requests, and addresses concerns the panel may have with regards to the accreditation application.

After completing its review, the accreditation panel votes to award or deny accreditation or continue the agency in Candidate or Correspondent Status or place the agency on probation. When an agency receives a three-year accreditation award, a certificate with the effective date of the award is presented to the agency representative.

The Board of Commissioners may stipulate additional requirements for accreditation if, in its opinion, conditions exist in the facility or program that adversely affect the life, health, or safety of the staff or offenders. These requests are specific regarding activities required and timeliness for their completion. The panel advises the agency representative of all changes at the time the accreditation decision is made.

ACA and the Commission may deny accreditation for insufficient standards/expected practices compliance, inadequate plans of action, or failure to meet other requirements as determined by the Commission, including, but not limited to, the conditions of confinement in a given facility. In not awarding accreditation, the Commission may extend an agency in Candidate Status for a specific period of time and for identified deficiencies, if in its judgment the agency is actively pursuing compliance. Those agencies denied accreditation, but not extended in Candidate Status, may reapply for accreditation after 180 days. The agency receives written notification of all decisions relative to its accreditation following the accreditation hearing.

Accredited Status

During the three-year accreditation period, ACA requires that accredited agencies submit annual certification statements confirming continued standards/expected practices compliance at levels necessary for accreditation. The report should include the agency's progress on completing plans of action and other significant events that may affect the accreditation award. In addition, ACA may require accredited agencies to submit written responses to public criticism, notoriety, or patterns of complaints about agency activity that suggest a failure to maintain standards/expected practices compliance. The Association, at its own expense and with advance notice, may conduct on-site monitoring visits to verify continued standards/expected practices compliance or conditions of confinement.

Reconsideration Process

The goal of ACA's accreditation process is to ensure the equity, fairness, and reliability of its decisions, particularly those that constitute either denial or revocation of Accredited Status. Therefore, an agency may request reconsideration of any denial or revocation of accreditation. However, the reasonableness of ACA's standards, criteria, and/or procedures for accreditation may not serve as the basis for reconsideration.

A reconsideration request is based on the grounds that the adverse decision is (1) arbitrary, erratic, or otherwise in substantial disregard of the criteria and/or procedures for accreditation as stated by ACA, (2) based on incorrect facts or an incorrect interpretation of facts, or (3) unsupported substantial evidence.

The agency submits a written request for reconsideration to ACA staff within thirty days of the adverse decision stating the basis for the request. The Commission's Executive Committee reviews the request and decides whether there is sufficient evidence to warrant a reconsideration hearing before the Board of Commissioners. The agency is notified in writing of the Executive Committee's decision.

Revocation of Accreditation

An accredited agency that does not maintain the required levels of compliance throughout the three-year accreditation period, including continuous compliance with all mandatory standards/expected practices, may have its accreditation award revoked. The agency is notified of its deficiencies and given a specified amount of time to correct them. If the deficiencies continue, the Board of Commissioners may place the agency on Probationary Status for an additional stated period of time and require documentation of compliance. Should the agency fail to correct the deficiencies, the Board of Commissioners may revoke the agency's accreditation and request that the accreditation certificate be returned to ACA. An accredited agency that has had its accreditation revoked for reasons of noncompliance also may use the reconsideration process.

Reaccreditation

To ensure continuous Accredited Status, accredited agencies should apply for reaccreditation approximately twelve months before the expiration of their current accreditation award. Agencies have the option of being audited from individual accreditation files or operational files. For detailed information on reaccreditation, consult your ACA regional administrator.

The preceding information is provided as an overview of the accreditation process. Additional information on specific procedures and elements of the process is available from ACA's Standards and Accreditation Department.

Mandatory Expected Practices/Standards for APPFS

4-APPFS-APPFS-3A-22
4-APPFS-APPFS-3B-01
4-APPFS-APPFS-3B-02
4-APPFS-APPFS-3B-03
4-APPFS-APPFS-3F-02
4-APPFS-APPFS-3F-03

Total of Weights

Category	Number
Mandatory Standards/Expected Practices	6
Nonmandatory Standards/Expected Practices	167
Total	173

Performance-Based Standards Explained

The performance-based standards and expected practices included in this manual are the result of a new, major initiative undertaken by the American Correctional Association to improve the delivery of care to offenders within the correctional environment using the concept and the new template for performance-based standards. Conceived and developed by professionals, these revised standards, practices, and outcome measures will enable administrators and practitioners to not only monitor activities but also to measure over time the outcomes of their efforts.

More than five years in the making, the American Correctional Association unveiled its first set of performance-based standards in August 2000. Partially funded by the Bureau of Justice Assistance (BJA), U.S. Department of Justice, *Performance-Based Standards for Adult Community Residential Services*, 4th Edition is the prototype that will guide the eventual development of all ACA standards manuals.

I. The Basics

The Bottom Line — What's Different?

Table 1 describes the relationship between the elements of current standards and the new performance-based standards.

TABLE 1: Comparing the Elements of Performance-Based Standards, Previous ACA Standards and Accreditation Terms

NEW Performance-Based Element	Previous Standards Element	Previous Accreditation Element
Standard	None (new element)	None (new)
Outcome Measure	None (new element)	None (new)
Expected Practice	**Standard**	**Standard**
Comment	Comment	**Comment**
Protocol	None	**Primary Documentation**
Process Indicator	None	**Secondary Documentation**

When Is a Standard No Longer a Standard?

As Table 1 suggests, the biggest change in terminology is what we used to call "standards" all have been reclassified as "expected practices." The reason for this change reveals the fundamental difference between prior standards and ACA's new performance-based standards.

The drafters of these new Performance-Based Standards for Adult Probation and Parole Field Services, Fourth Edition, found that all prior standards described activities or practices that were prescribed for practitioners, but a performance-based standard describes a condition to be achieved and maintained. When the drafters looked for statements of conditions in other manuals containing standards, the closest they could find were phrases found in some of the goal statements that preceded each major section.

What Does This Mean for Accreditation?

The impact of performance measurement on the accreditation process will not be much different than that which exists today. Guided by a summary of significant incidents and a report that examines conditions of confinement, the Commission on Accreditation for Corrections regularly examines issues that affect the life, health, and safety of staff and offenders. The major difference is that the Commission now will be reviewing a wider range of performances to determine whether improvements have occurred.

II. The Fundamentals of Performance-Based Standards

ACA's performance-based standards are comprised of several elements:

- **GOAL STATEMENT** (one for each functional area)
- **PERFORMANCE STANDARDS** (as many as are needed to achieve the goal)
- **OUTCOME MEASURES** for each performance standard
- **EXPECTED PRACTICES** for each standard, and corresponding—
- **PROTOCOLS,** and
- **PROCESS INDICATORS**

These elements are defined and described in Table 2.

TABLE 2: Definitions of Terms for Performance-Based Standards

Element	Definition
Goal Statement	General statement of what is sought within the functional area
Standard	A statement that clearly defines a required or essential *condition* to be achieved and maintained. A performance standard describes a "state of being," a condition, and does not describe the activities or practices that might be necessary to achieve compliance. Performance standards reflect the program's overall mission and purpose.
Outcome Measure	Measurable events, occurrences, conditions, behaviors or attitudes that demonstrate the extent to which the condition described in the performance standard has been achieved. Outcome measures describe the consequences of the program's activities, rather than describing the activities themselves. Outcome measures can be compared over time to indicate changes in the conditions that are sought. Outcome measure data are collected continuously but usually are analyzed periodically.
Expected Practice (s)	Actions and activities that, if implemented properly (according to protocols), will produce the desired outcome. What we *think* is necessary to achieve and maintain compliance with the standard—but not necessarily the *only* way to do so. These are activities that represent the current experience of the field, but that are not necessarily supported by research. As the field learns and evolves, so will practices.
Protocol(s)	Written instructions that guide implementation of expected practices, such as: policies/procedures, post orders, training curriculum, formats to be used such as logs and forms, offender handbooks, diagrams such as fire exit plans, internal inspection forms.
Process Indicators	Documentation and other evidence that can be examined periodically and continuously to determine that practices are being implemented properly. These "tracks" or "footprints" allow supervisory and management staff to monitor ongoing operations.

The following diagram (Table 3) attempts to describe the functional relationships among the elements.

TABLE 3: Functional Relationship of Performance-Based Standards Elements

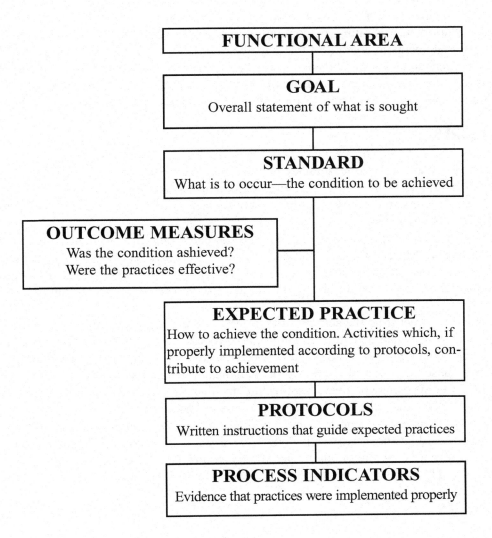

GOAL STATEMENT

Perhaps the least-appreciated element of the template, the goal statement attempts to establish an overall purpose for the standards in the functional area.

PERFORMANCE STANDARD

A performance standard is a statement that clearly defines a required or essential condition to be achieved and maintained. A performance standard describes a "state of being," a condition, and does not describe the activities or practices that might be necessary to achieve compliance. Performance standards reflect the program's overall mission and purpose and contribute to the realization of the goal that has been articulated.

In the beginning, the drafters of the new standards found it difficult to articulate clear and concise standards. The closer a draft standard came to meeting the definition of a performance-based standard, the simpler it seemed to appear. In drafting the new performance-based standards, the committee was constantly fighting the urge to describe an activity rather than to identify the overarching purpose for the activity. During many of the working group meetings, it was common for the proposer of a standard to be met with the response "Why?" While often frustrating, by continuing to ask the "why" question, the drafters were able to identify the basic statements of conditions that must be defined through performance standards.

Because performance standards are so fundamental and basic, it is less likely that they will require frequent revision. But as the field continues to learn from experience, it is predicted, and even hoped, that the expected practices that are prescribed to achieve compliance with standards will continue to evolve.

OUTCOME MEASURES

Outcome measures are quantifiable (measurable) events, occurrences, conditions, behaviors, or attitudes that demonstrate the extent to which the condition described in the corresponding performance standard has been achieved. Outcome measures describe the consequences of the organization's activities, rather than describing the activities themselves.

Because outcome measures are quantifiable, they can be compared over time to indicate changes in the conditions that are sought. Measurable outcome data are collected continuously but are usually analyzed periodically. The first time you measure an outcome, you establish a point of reference. By comparing the next measurement (weeks or months later), you can identify progress, or lack of progress toward the desired outcome.

Outcome measures are distinct from the activities of a program. For example, counting the number of vaccinations given to inmates is not an outcome measure (it is a process indicator), but measuring the incidence of disease in the inmate population is an outcome measure. Also, the number of inmates who were provided with substance abuse treatment would be a process indicator, where the number of inmates who pass drug screening tests would be an outcome measure. Outcome measures should be expressed as a ratio whenever possible—such as the number of walk-aways per offender bed-days.

Most performance standards have several outcome measures that may be used to determine if the condition described in the standard has been achieved. Conversely, a single outcome measure might be used to ascertain compliance for more than one standard. Outcome measures look at the bigger picture, by asking "what actually happened?"

EXPECTED PRACTICES

Expected practices are actions and activities that, if implemented properly (according to protocols), will produce the desired outcome—achievement of the condition described in the standard.

Expected practices represent what the practitioners believe is necessary to achieve and maintain compliance with the standard—but may not be the only way to achieve compliance. These activities represent the best thinking of the field, supported by experience, but often are not founded on research. As conditions change and as we learn from our experience, we expect practices to evolve.

It is arguable that expected practices should be changed over time to reflect our growing body of knowledge and experience. On the other hand, it is likely that we will see much less change with the overarching performance standards, which are more basic and fundamental.

PROTOCOLS

Protocols are written instructions and formats that guide implementation of expected practices, such as:

- policies and procedures
- post orders
- training curriculums
- formats to be used, such logs and forms
- diagrams such as fire exit plans
- internal inspection forms

Protocols provide a map to guide the proper implementation of expected practices. Protocols describe, usually in great detail, how to implement activities that are described in expected practices.

PROCESS INDICATORS

Process indicators can be used frequently—even continuously—to monitor activities and practices. But process indicators are not an "end" in and of themselves—they just tell if the expected practices are being implemented.

III. More About Outcome Measures and Process Indicators

Understanding the difference between outcome measures and process indicators can be difficult.

Process indicators relate directly to expected practices. Process indicators tell you if practices are consistently implemented according to protocols. For example, several expected practices address the provision of substance abuse services to offenders. Process indicators can establish if measured activities—such as screening, assessment, and therapy—were actually delivered to offenders but it is the outcome measures, such as the results of drug tests, that determine whether offender substance abuse patterns were positively affected.

Most of the process indicators referenced in this manual refer to written documentation that can be consulted "after the fact." In addition to these "footprints" that are left by an organization, implementation of expected practices may be confirmed during on-site inspection activities such as observation or interviews (with staff, volunteers, offenders, and others).

These additional activities (observations and interviews) are also a central part of ACA's accreditation process, comprising much of the work that is conducted on-site during audits. Accreditation participants also will recognize many of the protocols described in this manual as the "primary documentation" required by ACA as part of the accreditation process. Similarly, many of the process indicators cited are currently used as "secondary documentation" by the Commission on Accreditation for Corrections.

Observation and interview activities are usually suggested only when other methods are not possible. Observation, interview, and measurement rely on an on-site "single point in time" activity, while the other methods have the ability to examine practices randomly, over a longer period of time.

Outcome measures look at the "bottom line." Were expected practices properly implemented? Was the desired condition or state being described in the performance standard achieved?

There are three basic ways to express outcome measures:

- As <u>rates</u> (the frequency of an occurrence over time)
- As <u>ratios</u> (comparing two numbers as a fraction or decimal, such as the number of offenders diagnosed with hepatitis divided by the average daily population) or

- As <u>proportions</u> (the relation of a part to the whole, such as the number of offender grievances found in favor of the offender divided by the total number of grievances filed). A percentage is a proportion multiplied by 100.

You rarely will find an outcome measure that calls for simply counting an event or occurrence. We believe that usually outcome measures should include a numerator and a denominator if they are to be useful as management tools.

Whenever possible, the drafters have tried to use denominators that reflect the volume of activity. Therefore, it is preferable to divide by the average daily population rather than simply counting the number of events per month. The total numbers of hours worked by inmate workers during the past twelve months is used, whenever appropriate. In a few instances, other denominators have been used. What do the numbers mean after the math is done? They provide a starting point for analyzing and assessing the organization.

The first time outcome measures are generated, they will not mean much, but their value grows every time they are measured. The second time outcomes are measured, current outcomes can be compared to those that were measured in the past. In this way, outcome measures become a valuable management tool. Over time, the series of outcome measures that are calculated can provide invaluable insight into various aspects of the operation. Sometimes, they will provide important "red flags" that identify troubling trends.

IV. What Does This Mean for Accreditation?

Agencies applying for accreditation under the performance-based format now will be required not only to submit the data from the outcome measures at the time of their audit, they also will be required to submit the data yearly in conjunction with their annual certification report. The original outcome measures will be used to establish baseline data and each year's ensuing report will be added to the database. As each agency is considered for reaccreditation, the Commission on Accreditation for Corrections will review the historical data over the three-year period as well as the data generated by the most recent audit. When the Commission renders an accreditation decision, the outcome measures and the levels of compliance with the expected practices will be considered as part of the totality of conditions of the system.

1. COMMUNITY INDEX

Goal: A safe and vital community where the public feels safe and lives free of the risk of crime.

INDEX: 4-APPFS-1 COMMUNITY			
PERFORMANCE-BASED STANDARD: COMMUNITY PROTECTION 1A. Members of the community are protected from crime.			
Expected Practice	**4-APPFS Number**	**3-APPFS Reference Number**	**Page Number**
Community Justice Define	4-APPFS-1A-01	New	3
Community Collaboration	4-APPFS-1A-02	New	3
Resource Development	4-APPFS-1A-03	3-APPFS-3148	4
Victim(s) Notification	4-APPFS-1A-04	3-APPFS-3195	4

INDEX: 4-APPFS-1 COMMUNITY			
PERFORMANCE-BASED STANDARD: SENTENCING RECOMMENDATIONS 1B. Sentencing recommendations promote protection of the public and lawful offender behavior.			
Expected Practice	**4-APPFS Number**	**3-APPFS Reference Number**	**Page Number**
Pre-Sentence Investigations	4-APPFS-1B-01	3-APPFS-3213	5
Resources	4-APPFS-1B-02	3-APPFS-3212	5
Minimum Required Data	4-APPFS-1B-03	3-APPFS-3211	5
Victim(s) Statement	4-APPFS-1B-04	3-APPFS-3214	6
Recommendations and Conditions	4-APPFS-1B-05	3-APPFS-3218	6
Sentencing Alternatiives	4-APPFS-1B-06	3-APPFS-3219	6
Supervisory Review	4-APPFS-1B-07	3-APPFS-3225	6
Process Review	4-APPFS-1B-08	3-APPFS-3215	7
Information Sharing	4-APPFS-1B-09	3-APPFS-3227	7
Confidentiality	4-APPFS-1B-10	3-APPFS-3226	7

INDEX: 4-APPFS-1 COMMUNITY

PERFORMANCE-BASED STANDARD: RESPONSIBILITY
1C. The agency is a responsible member of the community.

Expected Practice	4-APPFS Number	3-APPFS Reference Number	Page Number
Public Information	4-APPFS-1C-01	3-APPFS-3027 3-APPFS-3028	8
Citizen Complaints	4-APPFS-1C-02	3-APPFS-3030	8
Citizen Involvement and Volunteers	4-APPFS-1C-03	3-APPFS-3117	9
Volunteers Policies	4-APPFS-1C-04	3-APPFS-3118	9
Recruitment, Screening, and Selection	4-APPFS-1C-05	3-APPFS-3120	9
Orientation and Training	4-APPFS-1C-06	3-APPFS-3122	9
Volunteer Service Agreement	4-APPFS-1C-07	3-APPFS-3123	9
Protection from Liability	4-APPFS-1C-08	3-APPFS-3124	10

1. COMMUNITY

GOAL: A safe and vital community where the public feels safe and lives free of the risk of crime.

PERFORMANCE-BASED STANDARD: COMMUNITY PROTECTION

1A. Members of the community are protected from crime.

Outcome Measures:
(1) Number of offenders who were arrested for any new criminal offense in the past 12 months divided by the total agency caseload in the past 12 months
(2) Number of offenders who were convicted of any new criminal offense in the past 12 months divided by the total agency caseload in the past 12 months

EXPECTED PRACTICES

Community Justice Defined
4-APPFS-1A-01
(New)

The agency works with the community to define the concept and practice of community justice. The agency actively participates in partnerships with individuals, organizations, and agencies to prevent victimization, provide conflict resolution, and promote public safety.

Comment: Partnerships should be explored with the full range of "stakeholders" in the public and private sectors, including, but not limited to: criminal justice agencies and entities (law enforcement, prosecution, defense bar, judiciary, corrections); human service providers; victim(s)' organizations; advocacy groups; service organizations; all levels of government (elected officials, appointed officials, staff); business; education; health care; faith community; organized labor; employment and training agencies; and offenders' families.

Protocols: Written policy and procedure.
Process: Indicators: Documentation of collaboration with community (meeting notes, media articles, memoranda of understanding, letters, and so forth.)

Community Collaboration
4-APPFS-1A-02
(New)

The agency engages in collaborative problem-solving efforts with the community to promote public safety through the sharing of information (consistent with applicable law) and education.

Comment: None.

Protocols: Written policy and procedure. Information-sharing protocols. Data collection and analysis procedures and report formats. Public education curricula and resource materials.

Process Indicators: Reports. Documentation of sharing of information (meeting notes/minutes, correspondence, media coverage). Staff interviews.

Resource Development
4-APPFS-1A-03
(Ref. 3-3148)   **The agency supports efforts to develop community resources that prevent crime.**

Comment: Community resources may include intelligence sharing with law enforcement agencies, task forces, and neighborhood watch.

Protocols: Written policy and procedure. Crime prevention plan.
Process Indicators: Documentation of crime prevention activities. Documentation of offender reentry activities. Offender records.

Victim(s') Notification
4-APPFS-1A-04
(Ref. 3-3195)   **When an offender is under the supervision of the agency for a crime of violence, consistent with the law of the jurisdiction, and if the victim(s) requests, there is a system for providing notification to the registered victim(s) that includes, but is not limited to,**

- **prior to any type of hearing regarding the offender's sentence**
- **prior to any release from confinement or supervision of the offender**
- **immediately after the offender escapes from custody or supervision**

Follow-up notification is communicated to victim(s) when the offender is apprehended and returned to custody after an escape.

Comment: Custody may include halfway house, work release, treatment facility, or electronic supervision.

Protocols: Written policy and procedure. Notification procedures. Notification forms.
Process Indicators: Documentation of notification efforts. Staff interviews. Agency records (victim(s) notification logs).

PERFORMANCE-BASED STANDARD: SENTENCING RECOMMENDATIONS

1B. Sentencing recommendations promote protection of the public and lawful offender behavior.

Outcome Measures: None.

EXPECTED PRACTICES

Pre-Sentence Investigations
4-APPFS-1B-01
(Ref. 3-3213)

The pre-sentence investigation process is governed by written procedures.

Comment: None.

Protocols: Written policy and procedure. Pre-sentence investigation forms, formats and instructions.
Process Indicators: Offender records (pre-sentence investigation reports).

Resources
4-APPFS-1B-02
(Ref. 3-3212)

The agency provides resources to ensure the submission of pre-sentence investigations within the time frames ordered by the sentencing court.

Comment: None.

Protocols: Written policy and procedure. Agency staffing plan. Job descriptions.
Process Indicators: Pre-sentence investigation reports and court records. Offender records. Staff interviews.

Minimum Required Data
4-APPFS-1B-03
(Ref. 3-3211)

Pre-sentence investigations and reports provide the sentencing court with timely, relevant, and accurate data, so that it may select the most appropriate disposition.

Comment: At a minimum, pre-sentence investigations typically include the following information: victim(s') statement, if given by the victim(s); information on defendant, including prior record, educational background, family history, employment; and health; accurate restitution information; circumstances of the instant offense; and a proposed supervision plan (where applicable) for the defendant.

Protocols: Written policy and procedure. Pre-sentence investigation report forms, formats and instructions.
Process Indicators: Offender records. Interviews with court officials.

Victim(s') Statement

4-APPFS-1B-04
(Ref. 3-3214)

Victim(s) are contacted and a victim(s') statement is obtained, if the victim(s) elect to make a statement. The statement is contained in the pre-sentence investigation report.

Comment: None.

Protocols: Written policy and procedure. Pre-sentence investigation report forms, formats and instructions.
Process Indicators: Offender records (pre-sentence investigations). Interviews with victim(s).

Recommendations and Conditions

4-APPFS-1B-05
(Ref. 3-3218)

When expected by the court, recommendations are developed during the pre-sentence investigation and are included as part of the pre-sentence investigation and report.

Comment: The agency should adopt uniform conditions that may be recommended for some categories of offenders based on risk and needs.

Protocols: Written policy and procedure. Pre-sentence investigation report forms, formats and instructions. Uniform conditions. Description of available sentencing options.
Process Indicators: Offender records (pre-sentence investigation reports).

Sentencing Alternatives

4-APPFS-1B-06
(Ref. 3-3219)

Probation officers consider sentencing alternatives that match offender characteristics and needs and balance those needs with the primary mission of public safety.

Comment: None.

Protocols: Written policy and procedure. Pre-sentence investigation report forms, formats and instructions. Description of available sentencing options.
Process Indicators: Offender records (pre-sentence investigation reports). Staff interviews. Interviews with court officials. Interviews with prosecutors and defense bar.

Supervisory Review

4-APPFS-1B-07
(Ref. 3-3225)

All pre-sentence investigations and recommendations are subject to review and approval by a supervisor prior to submission to the court.

Comment: None.

Protocols: Written policy and procedure. Pre-sentence investigation report forms, formats and instructions.
Process Indicators: Offender records. Documentation of supervisor review of pre-sentence reports.

Process Review
4-APPFS- 1B-08
(Ref. 3-3215)

The pre-sentence investigation process is reviewed by the agency periodically in consultation with the court.

Comment: None.

Protocols: Written policy and procedure. Pre-sentence investigation report forms, formats and instructions. List of sentencing options.
Process Indicators: Documentation of administrator's review of investigations. Documentation of annual review of process.

Information Sharing
4-APPFS-1B-09
(Ref. 3-3227)

The agency promptly transmits pre-sentence investigations and reports to other criminal justice agencies, when the offender is transferred to them for confinement, consistent with applicable law and regulations.

Comment: None.

Protocols: Written policy and procedure. Transmission forms.
Process Indicators: Offender records.

Confidentiality
4-APPFS-1B-10
(Ref. 3-3226)

The confidentiality of pre-sentence investigations and reports is safeguarded consistent with law and privacy policies.

Comment: None.

Protocols: Written policy and procedure. Pre-sentence investigation report forms, formats and instructions. Copies of laws.
Process Indicators: Staff interviews. Offender records. Offender interviews.

PERFORMANCE-BASED STANDARD: RESPONSIBILITY

1C. The agency is a responsible member of the community.

Outcome Measures:
(1) Number of individual volunteers who provided services in the past 12 months
(2) Total number of volunteer hours delivered in the past 12 months.
(3) Total number of hours of community service delivered by offenders in the past 12 months
(4) Total number of hours of community service delivered by offenders in the past 12 months divided by the number of active offenders supervised in the past 12 months
(5) Number of community entities (committees, boards, and so forth) on which agency staff served in the past 12 months
(6) Number of presentations (speeches, panels, and so forth) provided to the community by agency staff in the past 12 months

EXPECTED PRACTICES

Public Information
4-APPFS-1C-01
(Ref. 3-3027, 3-3028)   **The agency has a public information process that fosters contact with the public and the media. Employees and media representatives are informed of the process.**

Comment: At a minimum, the process should include the following: the identification of areas in the agency that are accessible to media representatives; the contact person for routine requests for information; identification of data and information protected by federal or state privacy laws, or federal and state freedom of information laws; special events coverage; news release policy; and the designation of individuals or positions within the agency authorized to speak with the media on behalf of the agency.

Protocols: Written policy and procedure. Public information program/plan. Public information materials. Media notification list.
Process Indicators: Interviews with media representatives. Documentation of public and media contact. Staff interviews.

Citizen Complaints
4–APPFS-1C-02
(Ref. 3-3030)   **The agency investigates all citizen complaints regarding offenders. The complainant is informed of findings and, if appropriate, of action taken.**

Comment: None.

Protocols: Written policy and procedure. Investigation procedures and forms.
Process Indicators: Documentation of investigations and subsequent communication with complainant(s).

Citizen Involvement and Volunteers
4-APPFS-1C-03
(Ref. 3-3117)   **The agency provides for volunteer and intern involvement in programs.**

Comment: None.

Protocols: Written policy and procedure. Job descriptions. Volunteer/intern recruiting plan.
Process Indicators: Volunteer/intern rosters and time records. Staff interviews.

Volunteer Policies
4-APPFS-1C-04
(Ref. 3-3118)   **There is a system for recruitment, selection, training, term of service, termination of service, and definition of tasks, responsibilities, accountability, and authority of volunteers and interns.**

Comment: None.

Protocols: Written policy and procedure. Volunteer/intern selection procedures and forms. Volunteer/intern training curricula. Volunteer/intern orientation materials. Volunteer/intern job descriptions.
Process Indicators: Volunteer/intern records. Documentation of training.

Recruitment, Screening and Selection
4-APPFS-1C-05
(Ref. 3-3120)   **The agency recruits volunteers and interns from all cultural and socioeconomic segments of the community.**

Comment: None.

Protocols: Written policy and procedure. Volunteer/intern recruiting plan.
Process Indicators: Volunteer/intern records. Documentation of outreach activities.

Orientation and Training
4-APPFS-1C-06
(Ref. 3-3122)   **Prior to assignment, each volunteer and intern completes a documented orientation and/or training program.**

Comment: None.

Protocols: Written policy and procedure. Volunteer/intern training curricula. Volunteer/intern orientation materials.
Process Indicators: Volunteer/intern records. Documentation of training.

Volunteer Service Agreement
4-APPFS-1C-07
(Ref. 3-3123)   **Volunteers and interns agree in writing to abide by all agency policies.**

Comment: None.

Protocols: Written policy and procedure. Volunteer/intern agreement forms.
Process Indicators: Volunteer/intern records.

Protection from Liability
4-APPFS-1C-08
(Ref. 3-3124)

The agency provides against liability or tort claims in the form of insurance or other legal provisions valid in the jurisdiction, when authorized by law.

Comment: None.

Protocols: Written policy and procedure. Risk management plan. Copies of laws.
Process Indicators: Insurance policies and other documentation of coverage.

2. OFFENDER INDEX

Goals:
- Offenders become law-abiding, productive members of the community.
- Maintain order with clear expectations of behavior and systems of accountability while treating offenders fairly and respecting their legal rights.
- Improve offender behaviors and competencies that contribute to immediate and long-term success in the community.

INDEX: 4-APPFS-2 OFFENDER			
PERFORMANCE-BASED STANDARD: OFFENDER BEHAVIOR **2A. Offenders behave lawfully while under the supervision of the agency.**			
Expected Practice	**4-APPFS Number**	**3-APPFS Reference Number**	**Page Number**
Assessment	4-APPFS-2A-01	3-APPFS-3125	15
Objective Process	4-APPFS-2A-02	3-APPFS-3130	15
Placement	4-APPFS-2A-03	3-APPFS-3130 3-APPFS-3131	16
Contact	4-APPFS-2A-04	3-APPFS-3210	16
Victim Input	4-APPFS-2A-05	3-APPFS-3133	16
Targeted Interventions	4-APPFS-2A-06	NEW	16
Supervisory Strategies	4-APPFS-2A-07	NEW	17
Supervision/Service Plan	4-APPFS-2A-08	3-APPFS-3132 3-APPFS-3136	17
Plan Development	4-APPFS-2A-09	3-APPFS-3132 3-APPFS-3136	17
Plan Changes	4-APPFS-2A-10	NEW	18
Review/Re-Assessment	4-APPFS-2A-11	3-APPFS-3138 3-APPFS-3139	18
Supervision	4-APPFS-2A-12	3-APPFS-3137	18
Closing Summary	4-APPFS-2A-13	3-APPFS-3144	18
Early Termination	4-APPFS-2A-14	3-APPFS-3145	19
24-Hour Services	4-APPFS-2A-15	3-APPFS-3135	19
Interstate Compact(s)	4-APPFS-2A-16	3-APPFS-3180-3191	19

INDEX: 4-APPFS-2 OFFENDER

PERFORMANCE-BASED STANDARD: OFFENDER COMPLIANCE
2B. Offenders comply with conditions ordered by the sentencing court releasing authority.

Expected Practice	4-APPFS Number	3-APPFS Reference Number	Page Number
Conditions of Supervision	4-APPFS-2B-01	3-APPFS-3134	20
Investigation of Violations	4-APPFS-2B-02	3-APPFS-3157	20
Reporting Violations	4-APPFS-2B-03	3-APPFS-3156 3-APPFS-3158 3-APPFS-3159	20
Violation Warrants	4-APPFS-2B-04	3-APPFS-3173 3-APPFS-3174	21
Probable Cause Hearings: Timing	4-APPFS-2B-05	3-APPFS-3160	21
Probable Cause Hearings: Location	4-APPFS-2B-06	3-APPFS-3161	21
Postponement or Waiver	4-APPFS-2B-07	3-APPFS-3162	22
Notice	4-APPFS-2B-08	3-APPFS-3165	22
Hearing Officer	4-APPFS-2B-09	3-APPFS-3163 3-APPFS-3164	22
Preliminary Findings	4-APPFS-2B-10	3-APPFS-3166	23
Sanctioning Violations	4-APPFS-2B-11	3-APPFS-3167 3-APPFS-3168	23
Absconders	4-APPFS-2B-12	3-APPFS-3171	23

INDEX: 4-APPFS-2 OFFENDER

PERFORMANCE-BASED STANDARD: PAROLE AND POST-RELEASE SUPERVISION

2C. Parole and post-release supervision from prison (Applicable only to agencies that perform these functions)

Expected Practice	4-APPFS Number	3-APPFS Reference Number	Page Number
Information Request	4-APPFS-2C-01	3-APPFS-3194	24
Individual Release Plan	4-APPFS-2C-02	3-APPFS-3193	24
Reasonable Delays	4-APPFS-2C-03	3-APPFS-3199	24
Graduated/Partial Release	4-APPFS-2C-04	3-APPFS-3197	25
Community	4-APPFS-2C-05	3-APPFS-3200	25
Services	4-APPFS-2C-06	3-APPFS-3205	25

INDEX: 4-APPFS-2 OFFENDER

PERFORMANCE-BASED STANDARD: OFFENDER SUCCESS

2D. Offenders are successful in the community during their sentences and after discharge.

Expected Practice	4-APPFS Number	3-APPFS Reference Number	Page Number
Inventory	4-APPFS-2D-01	3-APPFS-3150	26
Education/Employment	4-APPFS-2D-02	3-APPFS-3152	26
Programs/Training	4-APPFS-2D-03	3-APPFS-3154	27
Drug Testing	4-APPFS-2D-04	NEW	27

INDEX: 4-APPFS-2 OFFENDER

PERFORMANCE-BASED STANDARD: CONDITIONS OF SUPERVISION

2E. Offenders comply with all conditions of the court or releasing authority.

Expected Practice	4-APPFS Number	3-APPFS Reference Number	Page Number
Compliance/Non-Compliance	4-APPFS-2E-01	NEW	28

INDEX: 4-APPFS-2 OFFENDER

PERFORMANCE-BASED STANDARD: OFFENDER RESPONSIBILITY
2F. Offenders take responsibility for their actions.

Expected Practice	4-APPFS Number	3-APPFS Reference Number	Page Number
Opportunities	4-APPFS-2F-01	NEW	29
Restitution	4-APPFS-2F-02	NEW	30

INDEX: 4-APPFS-2 OFFENDER

PERFORMANCE-BASED STANDARD: FAIRNESS
2G. Offenders are treated fairly.

Expected Practice	4-APPFS Number	3-APPFS Reference Number	Page Number
Discrimination	4-APPFS-2G-01	NEW	31
Grievance Procedure	24-APPFS-2G-01	3-APPFS-2G-02	31

2. OFFENDER

GOALS:
- Offenders become law-abiding, productive members of the community.
- Maintain order with clear expectations of behavior and systems of accountability while treating offenders fairly and respecting their legal rights.
- Improve offender behaviors and competencies that contribute to immediate and long-term success in the community.

PERFORMANCE-BASED STANDARD: OFFENDER BEHAVIOR

2A. Offenders behave lawfully while under the supervision of the agency.

Outcome Measures:
(1) Number of offenders who were arrested for any new criminal offense in the past 12 months divided by the total agency caseload in the past 12 months
(2) Number of offenders who were convicted of any new criminal offense in the past 12 months divided by the total agency caseload in the past 12 months
(3) Number of offenders who were discharged in the past 12 months divided by the number of offenders removed from supervision in the past 12 months (discharged and revoked). (Comment: "discharged and revoked" includes offenders successfully and unsuccessfully terminated from supervision)

EXPECTED PRACTICES

Assessment

4-APPFS-2A-01
(Ref. 3-3125)

The agency's mission statement affirms that the supervision program is to provide necessary services to the offender with the goal of reducing the probability of continued criminal behavior on the part of the offender.

Comment: None.

Protocols: Written policy and procedure. Mission statement.
Process Indicators: Staff interviews.

Objective Process
4-APPFS-2A-02
(Ref. 3-3130)

The agency has an objective assessment process that identifies offender programming needs, risk of reoffending, and level of supervision. There are provisions for regular review. The assessment process includes the following:
- **an initial assessment of each offender using a standardized and validated assessment tool**
- **additional assessments or evaluations**
- **personal interview with the offender**
- **development of objectives that address community safety and offender needs**
- **assessment or reassessment results are recorded in the case file and communicated with the offender**

Comment: Additional assessments or evaluations may include such things as mental health and substance-abuse-screening tools. Regular reviews should be consistent with the complexity of the offender's program and the length of supervision.

Protocols: Written policy and procedure. Assessment forms and procedures.
Process Indicators: Assessment records.

Placement
4-APPFS-2A-03
(Ref. 3-3130, 3-3131)

Offenders are placed in the appropriate supervision category within 45 days of their being placed on supervision. Offenders are reassessed, as needed, and reassessment reviews are documented in chronological order. Adjustments to the individual plan are made based on reassessment, and are made in accordance with the offender's performance in the community.

Comment: None.

Protocols: Written policy and procedure. Assessment forms and procedures.
Process Indicators: Assessment records. Offender records.

Contact
4-APPFS-2A-04
(Ref. 3-3210)

Upon receiving notification that a high-risk offender has been placed on community supervision, an officer initiates contact with the offender within two working days, and conducts an initial supervision interview within five working days or prior to release from confinement. An initial interview for all other offenders shall be conducted within 30 days of being placed on community supervision.

Comment: Agencies should determine what constitutes a "high-risk offender."

Protocols: Written policy and procedure.
Process Indicators: Offender records.

Victim Input
4-APPFS-2A-05
(Ref. 3-3133)

Consistent with law in the jurisdiction, policy defines when and how victim input is sought before a probation/parole officer requests the court or the releasing authority to add, remove, or modify any of the court-ordered special conditions of supervision.

Comment: None.

Protocols: Written policy and procedure. Victim(s) notification procedures and forms.
Process Indicators: Documentation of victim(s) notification.

Targeted Interventions
4-APPFS-2A-06
(New)

Offenders are provided with interventions targeted to factors that relate to their individual criminal behavior and attitudes.

Comment: None.

Protocols: Written policy and procedure. Offender case management and program planning forms and procedures.
Process Indicators: Documentation of program planning.

Supervisory Strategies

4-APPFS-2A-07
(New)

The agency supports supervision strategies and programs that have been scientifically demonstrated to enhance compliance with the court or releasing-authority-ordered conditions, and that reduce criminal behavior.

Comment: A growing body of research supports the use of "evidence-based practices." Some supervision strategies are more effective than others at changing offender behavior. With resources scarce, agencies should focus their efforts on those strategies most likely to be effective in promoting public safety and offender integration.

Protocols: Written policy and procedure. Offender case management and program planning forms and procedures.
Process Indicators: Documentation of program planning

Supervision/Service Plan

4-APPFS-2A-08
(Ref. 3-3132 and 3-3136) **An individualized supervision plan is developed for each offender. This plan is reviewed and approved by a supervisor. The offender receives a copy of the plan. The plan includes, as appropriate:**
- **conditions of supervision**
- **the appropriate level of supervision as determined by the offender's risk and need**
- **objectives to be met by the offender and the field officer**
- **services that address the offender's needs**

Comment: Higher risk offenders should have a more comprehensive supervision plan.

Protocols: Written policy and procedure. Assessment forms and procedures.
Process Indicators: Review of individualized supervision plans (offender records).

Plan Development

4-APPFS-2A-09
(Ref. 3-3132, 3-3136) **Staff and offender jointly develop and complete the individualized supervision plan within 60 days of disposition. The plan includes measurable criteria of expected behavior and accomplishments, a time schedule for achieving specific goals, and scheduled progress reviews. The plan is documented with staff and offender signatures.**

Comment: To provide individualized care, a personalized plan for each offender should be developed. Offenders should have input into planning, problem solving, and decision making related to their participation in the program.

Protocols: Written policy and procedure. Format for offender-supervision plan. Offender handbook/rules.
Process Indicators: Signed offender supervision plans. Offender records. Documentation of offender participation.

Plan Changes
4-APPFS- 2A-10
(New)

Any change in a individualized supervision plan is reviewed and discussed with the offender. This review is dated and documented by staff and offender signatures.

Comment: None.

Protocols: Written policy and procedure. Offender handbook/rules.
Process Indicators: Signed and dated review documentation.

Review and Re-Assessment
4-APPFS-2A-11
(Ref. 3-3138, 3-3139) **Agency policy governs the time frame for the review, re-assessment, and modification of the individualized plan and level of supervision. The offender's progress in achieving objectives is documented.**

Comment: Higher risk offenders should be reviewed more frequently than lower-risk cases. Supervisory review should be dependent on risk level or complications.

Protocols: Written policy and procedure. Assessment forms and procedures.
Process Indicators: Documentation of review with offender.

Supervision
4-APPFS-2A-12
(Ref. 3-3137)

When specific services ordered by the court or releasing authority are not available, field staff notifies the court or releasing authority and requests guidance.

Comment: None.

Protocols: Written policy and procedure.
Process Indicators: Offender records.

Closing Summary
4-APPFS-2A-13
(Ref. 3-3144)

A closing summary or a final progress report is prepared that summarizes the performance of the offender during the entire period of supervision. The closing summary or final progress report remains in the offender's supervision record.

Comment: None.

Protocols: Written policy and procedure. Format for final report/summary.
Process Indicators: Offender records.

Early Termination
4-APPFS-2A-14
(Ref. 3-3145) **If permitted by law, early termination may be recommended to the court or releasing authority, when there is compliance with the conditions of supervision.**

Comment: None.

Protocols: Written policy and procedure. Format for recommendation. Process
Process Indicators: Offender records.

24-Hour Services
4-APPFS-2A-15
(Ref. 3135) **Agency staff is available 24-hours a day. Offenders should be made aware of how to access the 24-hour services.**

Comment: Effective supervision of offenders requires that some level of services be available at all times.

Protocols: Policy and procedure.
Process Indicators: Agency records. Offender records.

Interstate Compact(s)
4-APPFS-2A-16
(Ref. 3-3180 - 3-3191) **The transfer of supervision of offenders to and from other jurisdictions is governed by policies that are in accordance with the Interstate Compact for Adult Offender Supervision.**

Comment: None.

Protocols: Written policy and procedure. Interstate Compact Agreement.
Process Indicators: Agency records. Offender records.

PERFORMANCE-BASED STANDARD: OFFENDER COMPLIANCE

2B. Offenders comply with conditions ordered by the sentencing court or releasing authority.

Outcome Measures:

(1) Number of offenders found in violation of a new criminal offense during the past 12 months, divided by the total agency caseload during the past 12 months.

(2) Number of offenders found in violation of a technical violation only during the past 12 months, divided by the total agency caseload during the past 12 months.

(3) Number of offenders who absconded during the past 12 months, divided by the number of offenders who were under active supervision in the past 12 months.

EXPECTED PRACTICES

Conditions of Supervision

4-APPFS-2B-01
(Ref. 3-3134)

Conditions of supervision are furnished in writing to offenders. Offenders are required to sign the conditions, indicating understanding and willingness to comply with them. The conditions are explained by an officer. If a communication problem (such as illiteracy or foreign language) prevents an offender from understanding the conditions, an officer assists in explaining the conditions. Conditions are translated to the language spoken by the offender.

Comment: Every effort should be made to provide the offender written conditions in the language spoken by the offender.

Protocols: Written policy and procedure. Form/format for conditions. Acknowledgement form.
Process Indicators: Offender records.

Investigation of Violations

4-APPFS-2B-02
(Ref. 3-3157)

All alleged violations of the conditions are investigated and the results are documented in the case record. Substantiated violations are reviewed by the supervisor or as indicated by agency policy.

Comment: None.

Protocols: Written policy and procedure. Violation forms.
Process Indicators: Offender records. Documentation that supervisor has reviewed violations.

Reporting Violations

4-APPFS-2B-03
(Ref. 3-3156, 3-3158
and 3-3159)

In accordance with law and with authorization of the court or releasing authority, agency policy dictates what types of violations must be reported to the court or releasing authority and what types may be resolved internally.

Comment: Serious crimes and other major violations should be reported to the court or releasing agency. The least egregious violations should allow for officer discretion.

Protocols: Written policy and procedures.
Process Indicators: Offender records. Staff interviews.

Violation Warrants
4-APPFS-2B-04
(Ref. 3-3174, 3-3173) **Warrants for the arrest and detention of offenders are only requested upon adequate evidence of:**
- **serious and/or repetitive violation of the conditions; or**
- **commission of a new offense, or**
- **risk to public safety posed by the offender's continued presence in the community.**

Comment: None.

Protocols: Written policy and procedure.
Process Indicators: Offender records.

Probable Cause Hearings: Timing
4-APPFS-2B-05
(Ref. 3-3160)

When an offender is arrested and detained on a probation or parole warrant, or the warrant is lodged as a detainer on pending criminal charges, a probable cause hearing (PCH) is held within 14 calendar days of the arrest or lodging of the detainer. The probable cause hearing is not required if there has been a conviction or finding of probable cause by a court on the new charge.

Comment: None.

Protocols: Written policy and procedure.
Process Indicators: Offender records. Agency records.

Probable Cause Hearings: Location
4-APPFS-2B-06
(Ref. 3-3161)

The probable cause hearing is held in or near the community where the offense is alleged to have occurred, or where the offender was taken into custody.

Comment: None.

Protocols: Written policy and procedure.
Process Indicators: Agency records. Offender records.

Postponement or Waiver
4-APPFS-2B-07
(Ref. 3-3162)

The probable cause hearing may be postponed for good cause. The offender may waive the hearing if informed of due process rights pertaining to the hearing and the consequences of the waiver.

Comment: None.

Protocols: Written policy and procedure. Waiver form.
Process Indicators: Offender records. Agency records.

Notice
4-APPFS-2B-08
(Ref. 3-3165)

The offender is notified in writing of the probable cause hearing at least three days in advance. The notice includes the time and place of the hearing, and the offender's right to:
- disclosure of evidence
- present evidence and favorable witnesses
- confront adverse witnesses
- effective assistance of counsel, appointed if indigent
- request postponement of the hearing

Comment: Every effort should be made to provide the offender written hearing documentation in the language spoken by the offender.

Protocols: Written policy and procedure. Probable cause hearing notice form.
Process Indicators: Offender records. Agency records.

Hearing Officer
4-APPFS-2B-09
(Ref. 3-3163, 3-3164)

Administrative staff or a field officer may, at the request of the releasing authority, conduct the probable cause hearing and make findings as to the probable cause for revocation.

Comment: Preferably, the individual conducting the hearing has no prior involvement with the case, with the understanding that this may not be possible in smaller departments.

Protocols: Written policy and procedure.
Process Indicators: Agency records.

Preliminary Findings
4-APPFS-2B-10
(Ref. 3-3166)

The hearing officer conducting the probable cause hearing determines whether there is probable cause to revoke and hold the offender for final processing. When authorized by the releasing authority, the hearing officer may make the provisional revocation decision, or may report the findings and make a recommendation to the releasing authority. The hearing officer issues a verbal decision or recommendation immediately after the hearing and provides a written notice of the decision to the offender within 21 days of the hearing.

Comment: None.

Protocols: Written policy and procedure. Probable cause hearing decision notice form.
Process Indicators: Offender records. Agency records.

Sanctioning Violations
4-APPFS-2B-11
(Ref. 3-3167, 3-3168)

When violations occur, alternatives to revocation and incarceration are considered and used to the extent that public safety allows.

Comment: None.

Protocols: Written policy and procedure. List of alternatives.
Process Indicators: Offender records. Agency records. Staff interviews.

Absconders
4-APPFS-2B-12
(Ref. 3-3171)

When permitted by law, absconders who have committed no new crimes and who do not pose an undue public safety risk, may be continued under supervision in the community.

Comment: None.

Protocols: Written policy and procedure.
Process Indicators: Offender records. Agency records.

PERFORMANCE-BASED STANDARD: PAROLE AND POST-RELEASE SUPERVISION

2C. Parole and post-release supervision from prison (Applicable only to agencies that perform these functions)

Outcome Measures: None.

EXPECTED PRACTICES

Information Request
4-APPFS-2C-01
(Ref. 3-3194)

The supervising agency requests pertinent information about a prospective releasee in advance of the release date.

Comment: None.

Protocols: Written policy and procedure. Releasee notification procedures.
Process Indicators: Agency records (requests for information). Offender records.

Individual Release Plan
4-APPFS-2C-02
(Ref. 3-3193)

As permitted by law, agency policy specifies that no inmate is released until the agency has verified the individual plan for the inmate's release. The plan is reviewed and approved by the supervisor.

Comment: None.

Protocols: Written policy and procedure. Format for individual plan.
Process Indicators: Offender records. Agency records.

Reasonable Delays
4-APPFS-2C-03
(Ref. 3-3199)

Supervising officers may approve releasees' reasonable delays en route to approved programs.

Comment: None.

Protocols: Written policy and procedure.
Process Indicators: Offender records.

Graduated or Partial Release

4-APPFS-2C-04
(Ref. 3-3197)

The supervising agency participates in programs that include provisions for graduated or partial release, when allowable.

Comment: None.

Protocols: Written policy and procedure.
Process Indicators: Offender records.

Community

4-APPFS-2C-05
(Ref. 3-3200)

The supervising agency encourages the use of community residential centers for pre-release programs and for crisis situations.

Comment: None.

Protocols: Written policy and procedure. Agency budget.
Process Indicators: Financial records. Offender records.

Services

4-APPFS-2C-06
(Ref. 3-3205)

The supervising agency provides assistance and services to offenders who have been discharged and who request such help.

Comment: None.

Protocols: Written policy and procedure.
Process Indicators: Offender records. Offender interviews.

PERFORMANCE-BASED STANDARD: OFFENDER SUCCESS
2D. Offenders are successful in the community during their sentences and after discharge.

Outcome Measures:

(1) Number of offenders who were employed on a specified day in the past 12 months (single day count), divided by the total agency active caseload on that day

(2) Number of offenders who were employed upon discharge in the past 12 months divided by the number of offenders discharged in the past 12 months

(3) Number of offender substance abuse tests for which the results were negative in the past 12 months divided by the number of tests administered in the past 12 months

(4) Number of offenders who showed improvement as measured by an objective assessment instrument prior to release from supervision in the past 12 months divided by the total number of active offenders in the past 12 months (improvement from initial assessment to final assessment)

(5) Number of offenders referred for drug treatment in the past 12 months, divided by the number of offenders who successfully completed drug treatment in the past 12 months.

(6) Number of offenders referred to education programs in the past 12 months

(7) Number of offenders referred to behavioral programs in the past 12 months, divided by the number of offenders successfully completing behavioral programs in the past 12 months

EXPECTED PRACTICES

Inventory
4-APPFS-2D-01
(Ref. 3-3150)

The agency maintains a current inventory of community agencies that provide financial and other assistance to offenders. This inventory is readily available to field staff and offenders.

Comment: None.

Protocols: Written policy and procedure. Agency inventory. Evaluation criteria.
Process Indicators: Observation. Agency records. Staff interviews.

Education/Employment
4-APPFS-2D-02
(Ref. 3-3152)

The agency devotes specific resources to assist employable offenders in finding suitable employment.

Comment: Since employment is correlated with reduced offending, agencies should assist offenders who are able to work in finding employment.

Protocols: Written policy and procedure. Agency inventory.
Process Indicators: Observation. Agency records. Staff interviews.

Programs/Training
4-APPFS-2D-03
(Ref. 3-3154)

The agency supports the enrollment and support of offenders in educational programs and vocational training.

Comment: None

Protocols: Written policy and procedure. Agency inventory.
Process Indicators: Observation. Agency records. Staff interviews.

Drug Testing
4-APPFS-2D-04
(New)

If the agency conducts drug testing, policies are provided for collecting, processing, and disposing of samples, interpreting results, and responding to violations. The policy should include chain-of-custody and preservation-of-evidence procedures.

Comment: None.

Protocols: Written policy and procedure. Written instructions.
Process Indicators: Offender records.

PERFORMANCE-BASED STANDARD: CONDITIONS OF SUPERVISION

2E. Offenders comply with all conditions of the court or releasing authority.

Outcome Measures:
(1) Number of offenders who had "stay away from" or "no contact with" or "no violence toward" orders in the past 12 months, divided by the number of offenders who violated these orders in the past 12 months
(2) Amount of restitution collected in the past 12 months
(3) Amount of restitution ordered in the past 12 months
(4) Number of offenders whose cases were closed with total restitution paid in the past 12 months divided by the number of offenders whose cases were closed with restitution ordered in the past 12 months

EXPECTED PRACTICES

Compliance/Non-Compliance
4-APPFS-2E-01
(New)

> **The agency has a series of graduated responses to address compliance and non-compliance with conditions of supervision. These include proportionate incentives for compliance and sanctions for non-compliance with conditions of supervision.**
>
> *Comment*: None.
>
> *Protocols*: Written policy and procedure. Offender handbook/rules.
> *Process Indicators*: Offender interviews. Offender records.

PERFORMANCE-BASED STANDARD: OFFENDER RESPONSIBILITY

2F. Offenders take responsibility for their actions.

Outcome Measures:
(1) Amount of court costs, fines, and fees collected in the past 12 months, divided by the number of offenders who had court costs, fines, and fee obligations in the past 12 months

(2) Number of offenders whose cases were closed with total costs, fees, and fines paid in the past 12 months, divided by the number of offenders whose cases were closed with costs, fees, and fines ordered in the past 12 months.

(3) Total number of hours of community service performed by offenders in the past 12 months divided by the total number of offenders ordered to perform community service work for the past 12 months

(4) Total number of offenders who performed community service work in the past 12 months divided by the total number of active offenders supervised for the past 12 months

(5) Total number of offenders who participated in victim(s) awareness programs in the past 12 months divided by the total number of active offenders supervised for the past 12 months

(6) Number of offenders who had "stay away from" or "no contact with" or "no violence toward" orders in the past 12 months, divided by the number of offenders who violated these orders in the past 12 months

(7) Amount of restitution collected in the past 12 months

(8) Amount of restitution ordered in the past 12 months

(9) Number of offenders whose cases were closed with total restitution paid in the past 12 months divided by the number of offenders whose cases were closed with restitution ordered in the past 12 months

EXPECTED PRACTICES

Opportunities
4-APPFS-2F-01
(New)

The agency provides services and opportunities that encourage offenders to take responsibility for their actions. Opportunities are based upon victim(s) and community input and are fashioned in a way that seeks to ameliorate the harm done.

Comment: Opportunities may include paying restitution, performing community service hours, and paying court obligations such as fines and court costs.

Protocols: Written policy and procedure. Offender handbook/rules. Restorative justice program.

Process Indicators: Offender records. Documentation of restitution paid, community service provided. Documentation of satisfaction of offender obligations (for example, fines, court costs, family support).

Restitution
4-APPFS-2F-02
(New)

The agency places priority on services and opportunities that encourage offenders to make restitution to the victim(s) of their crime(s) and/or to the community.

Comment: None.

Protocols: Written policy and procedure. Restorative justice program.
Process Indicators: Offender records. Documentation of restitution paid. Documentation of community service provided.

PERFORMANCE-BASED STANDARD: FAIRNESS

2G. Offenders are treated fairly.

Outcome Measures:

(1) Number of offender grievances regarding discrimination in the past 12 months divided by the total agency caseload in the past 12 months

(2) Number of offender grievances regarding discrimination resolved in favor of offenders in the past 12 months divided by the total number of offender grievances filed regarding discrimination in the past 12 months

(3) Number of other offender grievances filed in the past 12 months divided by the total agency caseload in the past 12 months

(4) Number of other offender grievances resolved in favor of offenders in the past 12 months divided by the total number of other grievances filed in the past 12 months

(5) Number of adverse judgments or consent decrees against the agency by offenders in the past 12 months

EXPECTED PRACTICES

Discrimination

4-APPFS-2G-01
(New)

Agency policy prohibits harassment and discrimination of offenders based on race, religion, national origin, gender, sexual orientation, disability, or political views.

Comment: None.

Protocols: Written policy and procedure.
Process Indicators: Interviews. Grievances.

Grievance Procedure

4-APPFS- 2G-02
(Ref. 3-3179)

A grievance procedure that includes at least one level of appeal is available to all offenders. The grievance procedure is evaluated at least annually to determine its efficiency and effectiveness. The quantity and nature of offender grievances are aggregated and analyzed annually. All offenders are informed of the grievance program available to them at the time of the initial interview.

Comment: A grievance procedure is an administrative means for the expression and resolution of offender problems. Analysis of grievances allows the facility to identify problem areas and to take corrective action to prevent grievances.

Protocols: Written policy and procedure. Offender handbook/rules. Grievance procedures.
Process Indicators: Offender records. Documentation of grievances. Documentation of annual review and analysis.

3. AGENCY INDEX

Goal: Administer and manage the agency in a professional and responsible manner, consistent with legal requirements.

INDEX: 4-APPFS-3 AGENCY			
PERFORMANCE-BASED STANDARD: COMPETENCE, TRAINING, AND DEVELOPMENT 3A. Staff, contractors, interns, and volunteers perform duties properly.			
Expected Practice	**4-APPFS Number**	**3-APPFS Reference Number**	**Page Number**
Qualifications	4-APPFS-3A-01	3-APPFS-3049	40
Criminal Record Check	4-APPFS-3A-02	3-APPFS-3058	40
Physical Examination	4-APPFS-3A-03	3-APPFS-3059	40
Weapon Authorization	4-APPFS-3A-04	3-APPFS-3087-1	41
Orientation	4-APPFS-3A-05	3-APPFS-3082	41
Coordination/Supervision	4-APPFS-3A-06	3-APPFS-3072	41
Staff Development	4-APPFS-3A-07	3-APPFS-3073	42
Training Course	4-APPFS-3A-08	3-APPFS-3074	42
Curriculum	4-APPFS-3A-09	3-APPFS-3075	42
Annual Assessment	4-APPFS-3A-10	3-APPFS-3077	42
Training: Requirements	4-APPFS-3A-11	NEW	43
Agency Training Plan	4-APPFS-3A-12	3-APPFS-3076	43
Space and Equipment	4-APPFS-3A-13	3-APPFS-3081	43
Training Requirements	4-APPFS-3A-14	NEW	43
Administrative Staff	4-APPFS-3A-15	3-APPFS-3083	44
Support Staff	4-APPFS-3A-16	3-APPFS-3084	44
Professional Staff	4-APPFS-3A-17	3-APPFS-3085	44

INDEX: 4-APPFS-3 AGENCY

PERFORMANCE-BASED STANDARD: PROTECTION FROM HARM
3B. Staff, contractors, interns, and volunteers are protected from harm.

Expected Practice	4-APPFS Number	3-APPFS Reference Number	Page Number
Firearm/Less Lethal Weapon Policy **(MANDATORY)**	**4-APPFS-3B-01-M**	3-APPFS-3092	48
Firearm/Less Lethal Weapon Procedure **(MANDATORY)**	**4-APPFS-3B-02-M**	3-APPFS-3088	48
Weapon Care and Safety **(MANDATORY)**	**4-APPFS-3B-03-M**	3-APPFS-3089	48
Revocation	4-APPFS-3B-04	3-APPFS-3090	49
Health Notifications	4-APPFS-3B-05	3-APPFS-3091	49
Use-of-Force Training	4-APPFS-3B-06	3-APPFS-3093	49
Office Safety	4-APPFS-3B-07	NEW	49
Field Visits	4-APPFS-3B-08	NEW	50
Arrest	4-APPFS-3B-09	3-APPFS-3096	50
Recovery	4-APPFS-3B-10	3-APPFS-3170	50
Search/Contraband	4-APPFS-3B-11	3-APPFS-3177	50

INDEX: 4-APPFS-3 AGENCY

PERFORMANCE-BASED STANDARD: ETHICS
3C. Staff, contractors, interns, and volunteers are professional, ethical, and accountable.

Expected Practice	4-APPFS Number	3-APPFS Reference Number	Page Number
Drug Free Workplace	4-APPFS-3C-01	3-APPFS-3060	51
Code of Ethics	4-APPFS-3C-02	3-APPFS-3068 3-APPFS-3069	51
Confidentiality of Information	4-APPFS-3C-03	3-APPFS-3070	52

INDEX: 4-APPFS-3 AGENCY

PERFORMANCE-BASED STANDARD: EFFICIENCY
3D. The agency is administered efficiently and responsibly.

Expected Practice	4-APPFS Number	3-APPFS Reference Number	Page Number
General Administration	4-APPFS-3D-01	3-APPFS-3001 3-APPFS-3002	53
Single Administration Officer	4-APPFS-3D-02	3-APPFS-3003	53
Table of Organization	4-APPFS-3D-03	3-APPFS-3016	53
Policy and Goal Formulation	4-APPFS-3D-04	3-APPFS-3008	54
Goals, Policies, and Priorities	4-APPFS-3D-05	3-APPFS-3005 3-APPFS-3007	54
Annual Policy Review	4-APPFS-3D-06	3-APPFS-3048	54
Participation	4-APPFS-3D-07	3-APPFS-3005 3-APPFS-3006	54
Achievement	4-APPFS-3D-08	3-APPFS-3115	55
Monitoring and Assessment	4-APPFS-3D-09	3-APPFS-3023	55
Publication	4-APPFS-3D-10	3-APPFS-3024	55
Facilities and Equipment	4-APPFS-3D-11	3-APPFS-3004	55
Equipment Maintenance	4-APPFS-3D-12	3-APPFS-3025	56
Adequate Operating Facilities	4-APPFS-3D-13	3-APPFS-3026	56
Specific Qualifications	4-APPFS-3D-14	3-APPFS-3013	56
Minimum Qualifications	4-APPFS-3D-15	3-APPFS-3014	56
Academic Collaboration	4-APPFS-3D-16	3-APPFS-3018	57
Performance Reviews	4-APPFS-3D-17	3-APPFS-3061	57
Employment Evaluation	4-APPFS-3D-17	NEW	57
Career Advancement	4-APPFS-3D-17	3-APPF-3063	57

Legal Counsel	4-APPFS-3D-20	3-APPFS-3031	58
Fiscal Management	4-APPFS-3D-21	3-APPFS-3037 3-APPFS-3041 3-APPFS-3042	58
Budget Control	4-APPFS-3D-22	3-APPFS-3038	58
Minimum Fiscal Responsibilities	4-APPFS-3D-23	3-APPFS-3039	58
Budget Preparation	4-APPFS-3D-24	3-APPFS-3040	59
Cash Management	4-APPFS-3D-25	3-APPFS-3043	59
Independent Audit	4-APPFS-3D-26	3-APPFS-3044	59
Insurance and Indemnification	4-APPFS-3D-27	3-APPFS-3046	59
Case-Record Management	4-APPFS-3D-28	3-APPFS-3101	60
Record Maintenance	4-APPFS-3D-29	3-APPFS-3102	60
Record Formatting	4-APPFS-3D-30	3-APPFS-3103	60
Information Systems	4-APPFS-3D-31	3-APPFS-3104	60
Field Services Data	4-APPFS-3D-32	3-APPFS-3105	61
Quarterly Reports	4-APPFS-3D-33	3-APPFS-3106	61
Sharing of Information	4-APPFS-3D-34	3-APPFS-3107	61
Research	4-APPFS-3D-35	3-APPFS-3109	61
Conduct of Research	4-APPFS-3D-36	3-APPFS-3110	62
Project Review	4-APPFS-3D-37	3-APPFS-3111 3-APPFS-3112 3-APPFS-3113	62
Written Definition of Recidivism	4-APPFS-3D-38	3-APPFS-3114	62

INDEX: 4-APPFS-3 AGENCY

PERFORMANCE-BASED STANDARD: WORKING CONDITIONS
3E. Staff, contractors, interns, and volunteers are treated fairly.

Expected Practice	4-APPFS Number	3-APPFS Reference Number	Page Number
Working Conditions	4-APPFS-3E-01	NEW	63
Personnel Policy Manual	4-APPFS-3E-02	3-APPFS-3047	63
Equal Employment Opportunity	4-APPFS-3E-03	3-APPFS-3051	64
Unilateral Equal Employment Opportunity	4-APPFS-3E-04	3-APPFS-3052	64
Sexual Harassment	4-APPFS-3E-05	3-APPFS-3053	64
Unlawful Discrimination	4-APPFS-3E-06	3-APPFS-3053	65
Qualified Ex-Offenders	4-APPFS-3E-07	3-APPFS-3054	65
Selection and Promotion	4-APPFS-3E-08	3-APPFS-3055	65
Hiring	4-APPFS-3E-09	3-APPFS-3056	65
Compensation and Benefits	4-APPFS-3E-10	3-APPFS-3064	66
Expenses	4-APPFS-3E-11	3-APPFS-3065	66
Personnel Files	4-APPFS-3E-12	3-APPFS-3066	66
Access to Information	4-APPFS-3E-13	3-APPFS-3067	66
Employee Assistance Program	4-APPFS-3E-14	3-APPFS-3071	67
Grievances and Appeals	4-APPFS-3E-15	3-APPFS-3062	67
Employee Discipline	4-APPFS-3E-16	NEW	67
Termination or Demotion	4-APPFS-3E-17	NEW	67

INDEX: 4-APPFS-3 AGENCY

PERFORMANCE-BASED STANDARD: SAFETY AND SECURITY
3F. A safe and secure setting is provided for staff, contractors, interns, and volunteers.

Expected Practice	4-APPFS Number	3-APPFS Reference Number	Page Number
Emergency Analysis	4-APPFS-3F-01	NEW	68
Written Emergency Plan (MANDATORY)	**4-APPFS-3F-02-M**	NEW	68
Fire-Safety Inspection (MANDATORY)	**4-APPFS-3F-03-M**	NEW	68

INDEX: 4-APPFS-3 AGENCY

PERFORMANCE-BASED STANDARD: PROTECTION FROM HARM
3G. Staff, contractors, interns, and volunteers are protected from harm. Physical force is used only in instances of self-protection, protection of the offender or others, and the prevention of property damage.

Expected Practice	4-APPFS Number	3-APPFS Reference Number	Page Number
Physical Force	4-APPFS-3G-01	3-APPFS-3175	69
Incident Reporting	4-APPFS-3G-02	3-APPFS-3176	69
Transporting Offenders	4-APPFS-3G-03	3-APPFS-3097	70
Critical Incident Protocol	4-APPFS-3G-03	3-APPFS-3098	70

INDEX: 4-APPFS-3 AGENCY

PERFORMANCE-BASED STANDARD: VEHICLE SAFETY
3G. Agency vehicles are maintained and operated in a manner that prevents harm to the community, staff, and offenders.

Expected Practice	4-APPFS Number	3-APPFS Reference Number	Page Number
Annual Inspection	4-APPFS-3H-01	NEW	71
Repairs	4-APPFS-3H-02	NEW	71
Insurance	4-APPFS-3H-03	NEW	71

3. AGENCY

GOAL: Administer and manage the agency in a professional and responsible manner, consistent with legal requirements.

PERFORMANCE-BASED STANDARD: COMPETENCE, TRAINING, AND DEVELOPMENT

3A. Staff, contractors, interns, and volunteers perform duties properly.

Outcome Measures:
(1) Number of grievances against staff alleging improper conduct that were upheld or found valid in the past 12 months divided by the number of formal complaints against staff that were filed in the past 12 months
(2) Number of court decisions that found staff had acted improperly in the past 12 months
(3) Number of administrative decisions that found staff had acted improperly in the past 12 months
(4) Number of hours of professional development attended by staff in the past 12 months, divided by the number of full-time equivalent professional staff in the past 12 months

EXPECTED PRACTICES
Qualifications
4-APPFS-3A-01
(Ref. 3-3049)

An entry-level probation or parole officer possesses a minimum of a bachelor's degree or has completed a career development program that includes work-related experience, training, or college credits providing a level of achievement that is equivalent to a bachelor's degree.

Comment: None.

Protocols: Written policy and procedure. Job descriptions.
Process Indicators: Staff records.

Criminal Record Check
4-APPFS- 3A-02
(Ref. 3-3058)

In accordance with state and federal laws, a criminal record check is conducted on all new or prospective employees, contract personnel, interns, and volunteers to ascertain whether there may be criminal convictions that would affect job performance or delivery of services.

Comment: None.

Protocols: Written policy and procedure.
Process Indicators: Staff/contractor/intern/volunteer records.

Physical Examination
4-APPFS- 3A-03
(Ref. 3-3059)

Employees whose jobs involve use of force or include power of arrest receive a physical examination prior to job assignment.

Comment: None.

Protocols: Written policy and procedure.
Process Indicators: Staff records.

Weapon Authorization
4-APPFS- 3A-04
(Ref 3-3087-1)

All personnel authorized to carry a weapon other than a chemical agent receive a medical/physical evaluation, a mental health screening, and substance abuse testing prior to being issued such a weapon.

Comment: The term "mental health screening" refers to a review by a qualified, mental health professional of any history of psychological problems and examination of any current psychological problems to determine, with reasonable assurances, that the individual poses no significant risk to themselves or others.

Protocols: Written policy and procedure.
Process Indicators: Staff records.

Orientation
4-APPFS-3A-05
(Ref. 3-3082)

All new, full-time employees receive at least 40 hours of orientation before undertaking their assignments. Orientation includes at a minimum the following: orientation to the mission goals, policies, and procedures of the agency; orientation to the working conditions and regulations; office and field safety; employees' rights and responsibilities; code of ethics; an overview of the criminal justice system; and the particular job requirements.

Comment: None.

Protocols: Written policy and procedure. Orientation curriculum and materials.
Process Indicators: Staff interviews.

Coordination and Supervision
4-APPFS-3A-06
(Ref. 3-3072)

The agency's training program for all employees is specifically planned, coordinated, and supervised by a qualified employee at the supervisory level, and is reviewed annually.

Comment: None.

Protocols: Written policy and procedure. Job descriptions.
Process Indicators: Agency records. Documentation of annual review.

Staff Development
4-APPFS-3A-07
(Ref. 3-3073)

Training programs are based on needs assessment and a job/task analysis, incorporate measurable performance-based learning objectives, and are updated annually.

Comment: None.

Protocols: Written policy and procedure. Job/task analysis format.
Process Indicators: Agency records. Documentation of annual review.

Training Course
4-APPFS-3A-08
(Ref. 3-3074)

At a minimum, full-time agency training personnel complete a 40-hour train-the-trainers course.

Comment: Agency personnel whose primary duty is training should complete the train-the-trainer course. Subject matter experts asked to conduct training should be familiar with adult learning theory.

Protocols: Written policy and procedure. Training curriculum and materials.
Process Indicators: Staff records. Training records.

Curriculum
4-APPFS-3A-09
(Ref. 3-3075)

The training curriculum is developed based on clear, concise, and measurable written statements of intended learning outcomes. The content and instructional methods selected for a training program are consistent with the stated learning objectives, sequenced to facilitate learning, and incorporate strategies to evaluate the learning.

Comment: None.

Protocols: Written policy and procedure. Curriculum format.
Process Indicators: Agency records. Training records.

Annual Assessment
4-APPFS-3A-10
(Ref. 3-3077)

The agency administrator annually assesses personnel needs and plans for recruitment, training, and staff development.

Comment: None.

Protocols: Written policy and procedure. Recruitment, training and staff development plans.
Process Indicators: Agency records. Documentation of annual review.

Training: Task Analysis

4-APPFS-3A-11
(New)

The agency uses a statistically valid job/task analysis to determine the knowledge, skills and abilities needed to perform each job. This analysis is reviewed at least annually.

Comment: A job/task analysis identifies core tasks for each job within the agency. Core tasks are usually determined by the frequency that tasks are implemented and the criticality of each task (for example, the consequences of improperly performing the task).

Protocols: Written policy and procedure. Job/task analysis.
Process Indicators: Agency records. Documentation of annual review.

Agency Training Plan

4-APPFS-3A-12
(Ref. 3-3076)

The agency develops and implements a comprehensive training plan that describes the methods to be used to ensure that each staff member, intern, and volunteer has the needed knowledge, skills, and abilities to perform his or her assigned duties. The training plan is reviewed at least annually and is updated as needed.

Comment: The training plan should identify all aspects of training, including, but not limited to: curriculum development; training methods; instructor qualifications; trainee evaluation; and required resources.

Protocols: Written policy and procedure. Training plan.
Process Indicators: Training records. Documentation of annual review.

Space and Equipment

4-APPFS-3A-13
(Ref. 3-3081)

Space and equipment is available for required training and staff development programs.

Comment: None.

Protocols: Written policy and procedure. Facility plans/specifications.
Process Indicators: Observation. Staff interviews.

Training Requirements

4-APPFS-3A-14
(New)

All staff, including promoted or reassigned staff, receive the training necessary to ensure that they possess the requisite knowledge, skills and abilities before assuming assigned duties.

Comment: Staff highly skilled in specific areas may need additional training, so it is important to evaluate the knowledge, skills and ability of staff.

Protocols: Written policy and procedure. Training plan(s).
Process Indicators: Training records. Staff records.

Administrative Staff
4-APPFS-3A-15
(Ref. 3-3083)

All newly appointed supervisors and managers receive 40 hours of supervisory training within one year of their appointment. This training covers at a minimum the following areas: supervisory skills, general management; labor law; employee-management relations; relationships with other service agencies, and evidence-based practices for effective offender intervention. Forty hours of relevant training is received each year thereafter.

Comment: None.

Protocols: Written policy and procedure. Training curriculum and materials.
Process Indicators: Training records. Staff records.

Support Staff
4-APPFS-3A-16
(Ref. 3-3084)

All clerical/support employees receive 16 hours of training during their first year of employment and at least 16 hours of training each year thereafter.

Comment: None.

Protocols: Written policy and procedure. Training curriculum and materials.
Process Indicators: Training records. Staff records.

Professional Staff
4-APPFS-3A-17
(Ref. 3-3085)

All probation/parole officers and other professional employees receive 40 hours of training as soon as possible after their appointment but no later than one year, and 40 hours of training each year thereafter.

Comment: None.

Protocols: Written policy and procedure. Training curriculum and materials.
Process Indicators: Training records. Staff records.

Part-time Staff
4-APPFS-3A-18
(Ref. 3-3086)

All part-time employees working less than 35 hours per week receive training appropriate to their assignment.

Comment: None.

Protocols: Written policy and procedure. Training curriculum and materials.
Process Indicators: Training records. Staff records.

Evaluation of Training
4-APPFS-3A-19
(Ref. 3-3078)

The agency provides an ongoing formal evaluation of all pre-service, in-service, and specialized training programs, and completes an annual written evaluation report.

Comment: None.

Protocols: Written policy and procedure. Evaluation forms and procedures. Annual report.
Process Indicators: Training records. Staff interviews.

Staff Continuing Education
4-APPFS-3A-20
(Ref. 3-3099)   **Employees are encouraged to continue their professional development.**

Comment: None.

Protocols: Written policy and procedure.
Process Indicators: Staff records. Documentation of staff education (credit hours earned).

Professional Development
4-APPFS-3A-21
(Ref. 3-3100)   **The agency encourages employees to attend professional meetings, seminars, and similar work-related activities and provides administrative leave and/or reimburses employees for expenses connected with these activities.**

Comment: None.

Protocols: Written policy and procedure.
Process Indicators: Documentation of meetings and activities attended.

Use of Firearms or Less Lethal Weapons
4-APPFS-3A-22-M (Ref. 3-3087)
(MANDATORY)   **The issuance of, and authorization to carry, firearms and/or less lethal weapons is governed in writing. This includes the requirements for an approved training course that covers the use of, safety, and care of the weapon, and the constraints on its use. All personnel issued authorization to carry a firearm must demonstrate competency in its use at least annually.**

Comment: The word *annually* in the practice refers specifically to a 12-month period rather than a calendar year.

Protocols: Written policy and procedure. Training curriculum and materials.
Process Indicators: Staff records. Training records.

Self-Defense Training
4-APPFS-3A-23
(New)   **Officers are trained in self-defense techniques that are authorized by the agency. Training addresses the use of equipment authorized by the agency.**

Comment: None.

Protocols: Written policy and procedure. Training curriculum.
Process Indicators: Staff records. Training records.

Reference Services

4-APPFS-3A-24
(Ref. 3-3080)

Reference services are available to complement the training and staff development program.

Comment: The Agency should make every effort to ensure officers have access to outside information.

Protocols: Written policy and procedure.
Process Indicators: Observation. Training records. Staff interviews.

Staff Supervision

4-APPFS-3A-25
(Ref. 3-3126)

There is a written workload formula that allocates work to field staff and supervisors to accomplish its stated goals.

Comment: Caseload sizes will vary based on case types and job demands. Supervisor-to-staff ratios will be dependent on case types, staff experience and proximity of staff to supervisor.

Protocols: Written policy and procedure. Span of control criteria.
Process Indicators: Agency records.

Field Staff Supervision

4-APPFS-3A-26
(Ref. 3-3128)

Field staff who have caseloads report to a designated supervisor who is trained in supervisory functions.

Comment: None.

Protocols: Written policy and procedure. Job descriptions. Organizational chart.
Process Indicators: Agency records.

Field Supervision Review

4-APPFS-3A-27
(Ref. 3-3129)

Field supervision is systematically reviewed by the supervisor from both an administrative and case-management perspective. The reviews include case reviews, observation, and the provision of feedback to field staff.

Comment: Administrative management includes case files, data entry and written reports. Case management includes offender interaction and program referrals.

Protocols: Written policy and procedure. Review forms and procedures.
Process Indicators: Agency records. Offender records.

Support Services
4-APPFS-3A-28
(Ref. 3-3050)   **The agency provides the administrative and clerical support needed to accomplish its stated goals.**

Comment: None.

Protocols: Written policy and procedure. Agency staff roster.
Process Indicators: Staff interviews.

Channels of Communication
4-APPFS-3A-29
(Ref. 3-3021)   **The agency has a structured communication process that facilitates the timely exchange of information with, and between, all levels of employees.**

Comment: None.

Protocols: Written policy and procedure.
Process Indicators: Agency records. Staff interviews.

PERFORMANCE-BASED STANDARD: PROTECTION FROM HARM

3B. Staff, contractors, interns, and volunteers are protected from harm.

Outcome Measure:
(1) Number of injuries to staff requiring medical treatment in the past 12 months, divided by the total number of full-time equivalent staff in the past 12 months

EXPECTED PRACTICES

Firearms and Less-Lethal-Weapon Policy
4-APPF- 3B-01-M (Ref. 3-3092)
(MANDATORY) Where officers are authorized to carry firearms and/or less-lethal weapons in the performance of their duties, policy specifies those situations where agency personnel may carry and use these weapons.

Comment: None.

Protocols: Written policy and procedure.
Process Indicators: Agency records.

Firearms and Less-Lethal-Weapon Procedure
4-APPF- 3B-02-M (Ref. 3-3088)
(MANDATORY) If staff are authorized to carry firearms and/or less-lethal weapons, procedures govern their use, including the following:
- Weapons are subjected to stringent safety regulations and inspections
- Staff to whom weapons are issued follow procedures that specify methods for ensuring the security of weapons
- Staff are instructed to use deadly force only after other actions have been tried and found ineffective, unless the staff believes that a person's life is immediately threatened
- In the performance of their duty, staff only use firearms and/or less-lethal weapons approved by the agency and use them only as directed by agency policy

Comment: None.

Protocols: Written policy and procedure. Inspection forms and procedures. Training curriculum.
Process Indicators: Agency records. Staff records.

Weapon Care and Safety
4-APPF- 3B-03-M (Ref. 3-3089)
(MANDATORY) Prior to issuance of a firearm and/or less-lethal weapons, any staff member authorized to carry these weapons receives appropriate training. This training covers the use, safety, care, and constraints involved in the use of these weapons.

Comment: None.

Protocols: Written policy and procedure. Training curriculum.
Process Indicators: Staff records. Training records.

Revocation
4-APPFS-3B-04
(Ref. 3-3090)

A supervisor may revoke the authorization to carry a firearm and/or less-lethal weapon when reasonable cause exists. If the weapon belongs to the agency, it is seized and secured.

Comment: None.

Protocols: Written policy and procedure.
Process Indicators: Staff interviews. Agency records.

Health Notifications
4-APPFS-3B-05
(Ref. 3-3091)

Officers notify the agency of physical and pharmacological conditions that could affect the ability to perform their duties or carry a firearm and/or less lethal weapon safely. The agency takes steps consistent with law with respect to such disclosure and adopts and implements necessary procedures to safeguard such information.

Comment: It is important to realize that all staff may be at risk of injury or harm if physical and pharmacological conditions exist.

Protocols: Written policy and procedure.
Process Indicators: Staff records.

Use-of-Force Training
4-APPFS-3B-06
(Ref. 3-3093)

All officers are trained to implement the use-of-force continuum/matrix that is authorized by the agency. Training addresses the practices and use of equipment authorized by the agency.

Comment: None.

Protocols: Written policy and procedure. Training curriculum.
Process Indicators: Staff records. Training records.

Office Safety
4-APPFS-3B-07
(New)

The agency has an office safety plan that includes training, office configuration, and public contact.

Comment: Office configuration should optimize staff safety. Public contact should include how and when offenders and other visitors may be screened for weapons or other safety considerations.

Protocols: Written policy and procedure. Training curriculum.
Process Indicators: Observation of office layout.

Field Visits
4-APPFS-3B-08
(New)

The agency has a field safety plan that includes communication with the agency and/or other law enforcement agencies.

Comment: It is important to know the whereabouts of the officers at all times and that the officers have the ability to contact immediate assistance if needed.

Protocols: Written policy and procedure. Training curriculum.
Process Indicators: Agency records.

Arrest
4-APPFS-3B-09
(Ref. 3-3096)

A pre-arrest briefing is conducted prior to a planned arrest, with all officers and other law enforcement agencies participating in the action.

Comment: None.

Protocols: Written policy and procedure.
Process Indicators: Agency records.

Recovery
4-APPFS-3B-10
(Ref. 3-3170)

The types of action required to locate and recover absconders are specified by the agency and are disseminated to all staff members.

Comment: None.

Protocols: Written policy and procedure.
Process Indicators: Agency records.

Search/Contraband
4-APPFS-3B-11
(Ref. 3-3177)

Agency policy governs the search of offenders, the chain of custody, the disposition of seized items, and preservation of evidence.

Comment: Searches of offenders should comply with legal standards. All evidence seized should follow a prescribed chain-of-custody plan to ensure its value as evidence and to protect the agency and staff from allegations of wrongdoing.

Protocols: Written policy and procedure.
Process Indicators: Agency records.

PERFORMANCE-BASED STANDARD: ETHICS
3C. Staff, contractors, interns, and volunteers are professional, ethical, and accountable.

Outcome Measures:

(1) Number of disciplinary actions against staff in the past 12 months divided by the number of full-time equivalent staff positions in the past 12 months

(2) Number of staff terminated for disciplinary violations in the past 12 months divided by the number of full-time equivalent staff positions in the past 12 months

(3) [Where such testing occurs] Number of staff, contractor, intern, and volunteer substance abuse tests passed in the past 12 months divided by the number of substance abuse tests administered in the past 12 months

(4) Number of grievances against staff alleging improper conduct that were upheld or found valid in the past 12 months divided by the number of formal complaints against staff that were filed in the past 12 months

(5) Number of court decisions that found staff had acted improperly in the past 12 months

(6) Number of administrative decisions that found staff had acted improperly in the past 12 months

(7) Number of hours of professional development attended by staff in the past 12 months, divided by the number of full-time equivalent professional staff in the past 12 months

EXPECTED PRACTICES

Drug-Free Workplace
4-APPFS-3C-01
(Ref. 3-3060)
The agency supports a drug-free workplace for all employees. The agency's drug-free workplace policy includes, at a minimum, the following:
- **Prohibition of the use of illegal drugs**
- **Prohibition of possession of any illegal drug except in the performance of official duties**
- **The procedures to be used to ensure compliance**
- **The opportunities available for treatment and/or counseling for drug abuse**
- **The penalties for violation of the policy**

Comment: None.

Protocols: Written policy and procedure. Drug-free workplace policy. Training curriculum.
Process Indicators: Staff records. Staff interviews.

Code of Ethics
4-APPFS-3C-02
(Ref. 3-3068 and 3-3069)
The agency has a written code of ethics that it provides to all staff. At a minimum, the code:
- **Prohibits staff, contractors, interns, and volunteers from using their official positions to secure privileges for themselves or others**
- **Prohibits staff, contractors, interns, and volunteers from engaging in activities that constitute a conflict of interest**

- **Prohibits staff, contractors, interns, and volunteers from knowingly accepting any gift or gratuity from, or engaging in personal business transactions that would provide them a benefit not available to the general public or sexual relations with an offender or an offender's immediate family and**
- **Defines acceptable behavior in the areas of campaigning, lobbying, or political activities**

All staff, contractors, interns, and volunteers are held accountable for compliance with the code of ethics.

Comment: None.

Protocols: Written policy and procedure. Code of ethics.
Process Indicators: Staff records. Staff interviews.

Confidentiality of Information
4-APPFS-3C-03
(Ref. 3-3070)

The agency ensures confidentiality of information, consistent with state and federal laws and regulations. Staff, contractors, interns, volunteers and others who work with offenders are trained in and agree, in writing, to abide by confidentiality requirements.

Comment: Agencies are encouraged to develop a privacy policy regarding information sharing. The policy should include who has access to information that is shared between and among agencies.

Protocols: Written policy and procedure. Confidentiality policy.
Process Indicators: Staff records. Agency records.

PERFORMANCE-BASED STANDARD: EFFICIENCY

3D. The agency is administered efficiently and responsibly.

Outcome Measures:
(1) Number of material audit findings by an independent financial auditor at the conclusion of the last audit
(2) Number of objectives achieved in the past 12 months, divided by the number of objectives established in the past 12 months

EXPECTED PRACTICES

General Administration
4-APPFS-3D-01
(Ref. 3-3001, 3-3002) **Responsibilities and functions of the agency are specified by law or are administratively defined.**

Comment: None.

Protocols: Written policy and procedure.
Process Indicators: Agency records.

Single Administrative Officer
4-APPFS-3D-02
(Ref. 3-3003) **The agency is administered by a single administrative officer whose authority, responsibility, and function are specified by law or whose role is administratively defined by the parent organization.**

Comment: None.

Protocols: Written policy and procedure. Organizational chart. Job descriptions.
Process Indicators: Agency records.

Table of Organization
4-APPFS-3D-03
(Ref. 3-3016) **There is an organizational chart and description that reflect the current structure of authority, responsibility, and accountability within the agency and that is reviewed at least annually and updated, as needed.**

Comment: None.

Protocols: Written policy and procedure. Organizational chart.
Process Indicators: Agency records. Documentation of annual review.

Policy and Goal Formulation

4-APPFS-3D-04
(Ref. 3-3008)   **The agency administrator ensures that the preparation of a mission statement and long-range goals are reviewed at least annually and updated, if needed. The agency documents practical and specific plans to achieve its long-range goals.**

Comment: None.

Protocols: Written policy and procedure. Mission statement. Goals and plan.
Process Indicators: Agency records. Documentation of annual review.

Goals, Policies, and Priorities

4-APPFS-3D-05
(Ref. 3-3005, 3-3007)   **The agency administrator, with input from staff, is responsible for the formation of goals, establishing policies and priorities related to them, and translating the goals into measurable objectives for accomplishment by field staff. This planning process addresses the supervision and service needs of the agency.**

Comment: None.

Protocols: Written policy and procedure. Plan, objectives.
Process Indicators: Agency records.

Annual Policy Review

4-APPFS-3D-06
(Ref. 3-3048)   **The agency administrator reviews the agency's internal policies annually and submits recommended changes to the governing authority or parent agency.**

Comment: None.

Protocols: Written policy and procedure.
Process Indicators: Documentation of annual review and recommendations.

Participation

4-APPFS-3D-07
(Ref. 3-3006, 3-3005)   **All levels of staff participate in the development and review of the organizational mission, goals, policies, procedures, rules and regulations.**

Comment: None.

Protocols: Written policy and procedure.
Process Indicators: Documentation of staff participation.

Achievement
4-APPFS-3D-08
(Ref. 3-3115)

There is an internal system for assessing and documenting achievement of goals and objectives. Performance is reviewed at least annually, and program changes are implemented in response to findings as necessary.

Comment: None.

Protocols: Written policy and procedure. Internal monitoring system and forms. Inspection forms.
Process Indicators: Inspection/internal audit reports. Documentation of corrective actions taken.

Monitoring and Assessment
4-APPFS-3D-09
(Ref. 3-3023)

There is an internal system to monitor operations and programs at least annually through inspections and reviews by the agency administrator or designated staff.

Comment: None.

Protocols: Written policy and procedure. Internal monitoring system.
Process Indicators: Agency records. Documentation of annual review.

Publication
4-APPFS-3D-10
(Ref. 3-3024)

The agency administrator publishes a report at least biennially that includes goals, objectives, outcome measurements, programs, budget, major developments, and plans. The report also describes services furnished to the courts, releasing authority, offenders, and the community.

Comment: None.

Protocols: Written policy and procedure. Annual report format.
Process Indicators: Agency records (annual report).

Facilities and Equipment
4-APPFS-3D-11
(Ref. 3-3004)

Field offices are located in areas, with community input that are optimally accessible to offenders; places of residence and employment, to transportation networks, and to other community agencies.

Comment: Maximum involvement with the community is vital to the success of field supervision programs. The strategic location and appropriate design of facilities maximize staff performance and service delivery.

Protocols: Written policy and procedure.
Process Indicators: Observation. Staff interviews. Offender interviews.

Equipment Maintenance
4-APPFS-3D-12
(Ref. 3-3025)   **Staff is provided with equipment necessary to perform their assigned duties. All equipment is maintained in good working order and is replaced, as needed. There is a review of needs at least annually.**

Comment: None.

Protocols: Written policy and procedure. Equipment inventory.
Process Indicators: Observation. Agency records. Staff interviews. Documentation of annual review.

Adequate Operating Facilities
4-APPFS-3D-13
(Ref. 3-3026)   **The agency provides adequate facilities for all agency operations. Facility needs are reviewed at least annually.**

Comment: None.

Protocols: Written policy and procedure.
Process Indicators: Observation. Agency records. Staff interviews. Documentation of annual review.

Specific Qualifications
4-APPFS-3D-14
(Ref. 3-3013)   **The qualifications, authority, tenure and responsibilities of the agency administrator are specified by law, rules or regulations, or are otherwise administratively defined.**

Comment: None.

Protocols: Written policy and procedure. Administrator's authority.
Process Indicators: Agency records.

Minimum Qualifications
4-APPFS-3D-15
(Ref. 3-3014)   **The qualifications of the agency administrator are specified in writing by the appointing authority and include, at a minimum, a bachelor's degree, five years of related experience, and demonstrated administrative ability, and leadership.**

Comment: None.

Protocols: Written policy and procedure. Job description and qualifications.
Process Indicators: Staff records.

Academic Collaboration

4-APPFS-3D-16
(Ref. 3-3018)   **The agency collaborates with colleges and universities to provide educational opportunities, internships, and research.**

Comment: None.

Protocols: Written policy and procedure.
Process Indicators: Documentation of collaboration.

Performance Reviews

4-APPFS-3D-17
(Ref. 3-3061)

There is a written annual performance review of all employees that is based upon defined criteria and is reviewed and discussed with the employee. This review includes an appraisal of the knowledge, skills, and abilities that are required for each employee's job assessment, and identification of additional education or training that is needed.

Comment: None.

Protocols: Written policy and procedure. Performance review format and procedures.
Process Indicators: Staff records. Documentation of review with employee.

Employee Evaluation

4-APPFS-3D-18
(New)   **Employee performance is evaluated initially after six months of employment or job assignment and at least annually thereafter.**

Comment: Agencies who send new employees to an extended training academy may opt to begin the evaluation period after the employee begins his or her job assignment.

Protocols: Written policy and procedure. Employee evaluation plan and forms.
Process Indicators: Staff records.

Career Advancement

4-APPFS-3D-19
(Ref. 3-3063)   **Staff are made aware of opportunities for career advancement.**

Comment: None.

Protocols: Written policy and procedure.
Process Indicators: Staff interviews. Agency records.

Legal Counsel
4-APPFS-3D-20
(Ref. 3-3031)

Legal assistance is available to the agency for the purposes of formulating agency policy, advising on individual cases, interpreting case law, and representing the agency and staff, as required, before courts and other appropriate bodies.

Comment: None.

Protocols: Written policy and procedure.
Process Indicators: Staff interview. Agency records.

Fiscal Management
4-APPFS-3D-21
(Ref. 3-3037, 3-3041, 3-3042)

The agency budget is sufficient to enable the agency to meet its objectives, consistent with its mission and goals. Planning, budgeting, and program management functions are interrelated, and all are linked directly with objectives. Revisions are made, as necessary.

Comment: None.

Protocols: Written policy and procedure. Budget.
Process Indicators: Agency records (budget and budget development process). Staff interviews. Documentation of revisions.

Budget Control
4-APPFS-3D-22
(Ref. 3-3038)

The agency administrator is responsible for budget control and preparation, including expenditures and monitoring.

Comment: None.

Protocols: Written policy and procedure. Job description.
Process Indicators: Agency records.

Minimum Fiscal Responsibilities
4-APPFS-3D-23
(Ref. 3-3039)

The agency's fiscal activities and responsibilities include, at a minimum: internal controls, petty cash, indemnification, signature control of checks, and employee-expense reimbursement.

Comment: None.

Protocols: Written policy and procedure. Fiscal procedures.
Process Indicators: Agency records.

Budget Preparation
4-APPFS-3D-24
(Ref. 3-3040)   **The agency administrator participates in budget hearings and presents justification to support the budget request.**

Comment: None.

Protocols: Written policy and procedure. Budget format.
Process Indicators: Agency records (budget). Documentation of administrator's efforts to justify the budget request.

Cash Management
4-APPFS-3D-25
(Ref. 3-3043)   **When funds are collected from offenders, the agency administrator ensures the appropriate collection, safeguarding, and disbursement of all monies, consistent with law, policies, and directives. Staff is trained in these processes.**

Comment: None.

Protocols: Written policy and procedure.
Process Indicators: Agency records. Staff interviews. Documentation of annual review.

Independent Audit
4-APPFS-3D-26
(Ref. 3-3044)   **Internal audits of the agency's fiscal activities are conducted at least annually and independent audits are conducted at a time period stipulated by applicable law, but not to exceed three years.**

Comment: None.

Protocols: Written policy and procedure. Applicable law.
Process Indicators: Audit reports.

Insurance and Indemnification
4-APPFS-3D-27
(Ref. 3-3046)   **Employee insurance coverage and indemnification is provided and includes, at a minimum: workers' compensation, civil liability, liability for agency vehicles, a blanket bond, and group medical.**

Comment: None.

Protocols: Written policy and procedure.
Process Indicators: Insurance policies and other documentation of coverage. Staff records.

Case-Record Management

4-APPFS-3D-28
(Ref. 3-3101)

Record management practices include, but are not limited to: the establishment, use, content, privacy, security, preservation, and a schedule for retention of inactive case records and destruction.

Comment: None.

Protocols: Written policy and procedure.
Process Indicators: Agency records. Observation.

Record Maintenance

4-APPFS-3D-29
(Ref. 3-3102)

The agency maintains written and/or electronic records of case plan decisions, events, and activities regarding offenders.

Comment: None.

Protocols: Written policy and procedure. Record-keeping forms, formats, and protocols.
Process Indicators: Agency records. Offender records.

Record Formatting

4-APPFS-3D-30
(Ref. 3-3103)

Contents of case records are separated and identified according to an established format.

Comment: None.

Protocols: Written policy and procedure.
Process Indicators: Offender records.

Information Systems

4-APPFS-3D-31
(Ref. 3-3104)

The agency has access to, and uses, an organized system of information retrieval and review that is part of an overall management, planning, and research capacity.

Comment: None.

Protocols: Written policy and procedure. Information system forms, format and protocols.
Process Indicators: Agency records. Documentation of use of information for management, planning, and research.

Field Services Data

4-APPFS-3D-32
(Ref. 3-3105) **The agency administrator ensures that field services data is collected, recorded, organized, processed, and reported for information management purposes.**

Comment: None.

Protocols: Written policy and procedure. Data collection forms and protocols.
Process Indicators: Agency records. Documentation of participation and annual review.

Quarterly Reports

4-APPFS-3D-33
(Ref. 3-3106) **At a minimum, quarterly reports from those individuals in charge of the information system and research program are forwarded to the agency administrator.**

Comment: None.

Protocols: Written policy and procedure. Quarterly reports.
Process Indicators: Agency records (quarterly reports.)

Sharing of Information

4-APPFS-3D-34
(Ref. 3-3107) **Consistent with law and regulations, the agency collaborates with other justice system agencies and human service agencies in information gathering, exchange, and standardization. Agency policy dictates what information can be accessed and disseminated.**

Comment: None.

Protocols: Written policy and procedure.
Process Indicators: Agency records. Documentation of collaboration.

Research

4-APPFS-3D-35
(Ref. 3-3109) **The agency encourages research relevant to its programs.**

Comment: None.

Protocols: Written policy and procedure.
Process Indicators: Staff interviews. Agency records.

The following Expected Practices apply to agencies that conduct research.

Conduct of Research
4-APPFS-3D-36
(Ref. 3-3110)

The agency administrator and designated staff participate with researchers in deciding questions to be addressed, data to be gathered, and provide input into how that data should be presented.

Comment: None.

Protocols: Written policy and procedure.
Process Indicators: Agency records. Documentation of participation.

Project Review
4-APPFS-3D-37
(Ref. 3-3111, 3112, 3113)

The agency administrator reviews and approves all research projects prior to their implementation. The agency administrator approves a plan for the security and privacy of the information and data collection system, including verification, and access to and protection of the data. The plan ensures routine data protection. The method for dissemination of research findings is specified in writing.

Comment: None.

Protocols: Written policy and procedure. Information security plan. Dissemination plan.
Process Indicators: Agency records.

Written Definition of Recidivism
4-APPFS-3D-38
(Ref. 3-3114)

The agency has a written definition of recidivism, that is understood and used by all agency personnel.

Comment: None.

Protocols: Written policy and procedure. Definition of recidivism.
Process Indicators: Interviews with staff. Review of agency reports.

PERFORMANCE-BASED STANDARD: WORKING CONDITIONS

3E. Staff, contractors, interns, and volunteers are treated fairly.

Outcome Measures:
(1) Number of grievances filed by staff against the agency or its representative in the past 12 months divided by the number of full-time equivalent staff positions in the past 12 months.

(2) Number of staff grievances decided in favor of staff in the past 12 months divided by the total number of staff grievances filed in the past 12 months

(3) Total number of years of staff members' experience in the field as of the end of the last calendar year

(4) Number of staff terminated or demoted in the past 12 months divided by the number of full-time equivalent staff in the past 12 months

(5) Number of staff who left employment for any reason in the past 12 months divided by the number of full-time equivalent staff positions in the past 12 months

EXPECTED PRACTICES

Working Conditions
4-APPFS-3E-01
(New)

Staff, contractors, interns, and volunteers are provided with a safe, healthful, and comfortable work setting.

Comment: None.

Protocols: Written policy and procedure.
Process Indicators: Observation. Staff interviews.

Personnel Policy Manual
4-APPFS-3E-02
(Ref. 3-3047)

There is a personnel policy manual that covers the following subjects as a minimum:
- **Organizational chart**
- **Recruitment procedures**
- **Equal employment opportunity provisions**
- **Job qualifications, descriptions, and responsibilities**
- **Basis for determining salaries**
- **Benefits, holidays, leave, and work hours**
- **Personnel records**
- **Employee evaluation**
- **Staff development including in-service training**
- **Sexual harassment and hostile work environment prevention**
- **Promotion**
- **Physical fitness policy**
- **Retirement, resignation, and termination**
- **Laws relating to political activities**
- **Employee-management relations**

- **Disciplinary procedures**
- **Grievance procedures**
- **Insurance and professional liability requirements**

A copy of this manual is available to each employee, and changes are provided to all employees.

Comment: The manual may be made available to employees in various ways, such as giving a copy to each employee, placing copies in a staff library, and posting the manual on an internal website or intranet.

Protocols: Written policy and procedure. Personnel policy manual.
Process Indicators: Observation (availability to staff). Agency records.

Equal Employment Opportunity

4-APPFS-3E-03
(Ref. 3-3051)

There is a mechanism to process requests for reasonable accommodation to the known physical and/or mental impairments of a qualified individual with a disability, either an applicant or an employee. The accommodation need not be granted if it would impose an undue hardship or direct threat.

Comment: None.

Protocols: Written policy and procedure.
Process Indicators: Agency records.

Unilateral Equal Employment Opportunity

4-APPFS-3E-04
(Ref. 3-3052)

Equal employment opportunities exist for all positions.

Comment: None.

Protocols: Written policy and procedure.
Process Indicators: Agency records. Staff interviews. Staff grievances.

Sexual Harrassment

4-APPFS-3E-05
(Ref. 3-3053)

Policy and procedure specifically prohibits sexual harassment and specifies the process and designated staff to whom incidents of sexual harassment should be reported. Regular training is provided to staff.

Comment: None.

Protocols: Written policy and procedure.
Process Indicators: Staff interviews. Agency records. Staff grievances.

Unlawful Discrimination
4-APPFS-3E-06
(Ref. 3-3053)

Policy and procedure specifically prohibits unlawful discrimination and specifies the process and designated staff to whom incidents of unlawful discrimination should be reported. Regular training is provided to staff.

Comment: None.

Protocols: Written policy and procedure.
Process Indicators: Staff interviews. Agency records. Staff grievances.

Qualified Ex-Offenders
4-APPFS-3E-07
(Ref. 3-3054)

When permitted by law, employment of qualified ex-offenders is not prohibited.

Comment: None.

Protocols: Written policy and procedure.
Process Indicators: Staff records.

Selection and Promotion
4-APPFS-3E-08
(Ref. 3-3055)

Selection, retention and promotion of all personnel is consistent with law and governed by written procedure.

Comment: None.

Protocols: Written policy and procedure. Personnel policy manual.
Process Indicators: Agency records.

Hiring
4-APPFS-3E-09
(Ref. 3-3056)

Hiring and promotional practices are structured to select the best suited candidate. There are no artificial barriers to lateral entry.

Comment: None.

Protocols: Written policy and procedure. Personnel policy manual.
Process Indicators: Staff records. Agency records.

Compensation and Benefits
4-APPFS-3E-10
(Ref. 3-3064)

Salary levels and employee benefits for all field agency personnel are competitive with those of other components of the justice system as well as with comparable occupational groups.

Comment: None.

Protocols: Written policy and procedure. Compensation plan.
Process Indicators: Staff interviews. Compensation records. Comparative compensation data.

Expenses
4-APPFS-3E-11
(Ref. 3-3065)

Employees are reimbursed for all approved expenses incurred in the performance of their duties.

Comment: None.

Protocols: Written policy and procedure.
Process Indicators: Agency records.

Personnel Files
4-APPFS-3E-12
(Ref. 3-3066)

The agency maintains a current, accurate, confidential personnel record on each employee as allowed by law. Information obtained as part of a required medical examination (and/or inquiry) regarding the medical condition or history of applicants and employees is collected and maintained on separate forms and in separate medical files and treated as a confidential medical record.

Comment: None.

Protocols: Written policy and procedure. Format for personnel records.
Process Indicators: Staff records. Observation (provisions for confidentiality).

Access to Information
4-APPFS-3E-13
(Ref. 3-3067)

Employees have access to and are permitted to challenge information in their personnel file and have it corrected or removed if it is proven inaccurate.

Comment: None.

Protocols: Written policy and procedure.
Process Indicators: Staff interviews. Staff records.

Employee Assistance Program
4-APPFS-3E-14
(Ref. 3-3071)   **The agency provides an employee assistance program.**

Comment: None.

Protocols: Written policy and procedure. Description of employee assistance program.
Process Indicators: Agency records. Staff records.

Grievances and Appeals
4-APPFS-3E-15
(Ref. 3-3062)   **Employees have the right to request and exhaust grievance and appeals procedures as outlined in personnel policies, including an open and formal hearing, prior to their final termination or demotion or other adverse personnel action in accordance with applicable state/federal law or regulations to ensure fairness.**

Comment: None.

Protocols: Written policy and procedure. Personnel policy manual.
Process Indicators: Agency records.

Employee Discipline
4-APPFS-3E-16
(New)   **Employee disciplinary procedures include provisions for corrective action, progressive discipline, and limited due process.**

Comment: None.

Protocols: Written policy and procedure. Employee discipline procedure.
Process Indicators: Agency records. Staff records.

Termination or Demotion
4-APPFS-3E-17
(New)   **Consistent with applicable laws and regulations, termination or demotion is permitted only for a good cause and, if requested, subsequent to a formal hearing on specific charges.**

Comment: None.

Protocols: Written policy and procedure. Grievance procedure. Personnel rules and regulations.
Process Indicators: Staff records. Documentation from hearings.

PERFORMANCE-BASED STANDARD: SAFETY AND SECURITY

3F. A safe and secure setting is provided for staff, contractors, interns, and volunteers.

Outcome Measures:
(1) Number of fires that resulted in property damage in the past 12 months
(2) Dollar amount of property damage from fire in the past 12 months
(3) Number of code violations cited in the past 12 months

EXPECTED PRACTICES

Emergency Analysis
4-APPFS-3F-01
(New)

Emergencies are analyzed and the results used to initiate or revise policy and/or procedure to prevent future occurrences.

Comment: None.

Protocols: Written policy and procedure. List of key indicators for which data is collected. Data collection forms and procedures.
Process Indicators: Analysis of data. Records of actions taken to prevent future events.

Written Emergency Plan
4-APPFS-3F-02-M (New)
(MANDATORY)

There is a written emergency plan, that includes an evacuation plan, to be used in the event of a major emergency. The plan is reviewed annually and tested as provided in agency policy, and updated, if necessary. The plan includes the following:
- **Location of building/room floor plan**
- **Use of exit signs and directional arrows that are easily seen and read**
- **Publicly posted evacuation routes**

Comment: The evacuation plan also should specify evacuation routes, and provision for medical care or hospital transportation for injured offenders or staff.

Protocols: Written policy and procedure. Facility plan/specifications. Written emergency plan.
Process Indicators: Certification of emergency plan approval. Documentation of annual review.

Fire-Safety Inspection
4-APPFS-3F-03-M (New)
(MANDATORY)

The agency secures an annual fire-safety inspection by the authority having jurisdiction or other qualified person(s).

Comment: None.

Protocols: Written policy and procedure.
Process Indicators: Copy of annual inspection.

PERFORMANCE-BASED STANDARD: PROTECTION FROM HARM

3G. Staff, contractors, interns, and volunteers are protected from harm. Physical force is used only in instances of self-protection, protection of the offender or others, and the prevention of property damage.

Outcome Measures:

(1) Number of grievances against staff alleging improper use of force upheld or found valid in the past 12 months divided by the total agency caseload for the past 12 months

(2) Number of grievances against staff alleging improper use of force upheld or found valid in the past 12 months divided by the number of grievances alleging improper use of force filed in the past 12 months

(3) Number of court decisions against staff alleging improper use of force upheld or found valid in the past 12 months divided by the total agency caseload for the past 12 months

(4) Number of court decisions that found staff had used improper force in the past 12 months divided by the number of court decisions alleging improper use of force filed in the past 12 months

(5) Number of administrative decisions finding that staff used improper force in the past 12 months divided by the total agency caseload for the past 12 months

(6) Number of injuries that required medical attention resulting from staff use of force in the past 12 months divided by the total agency caseload for the past 12 months

EXPECTED PRACTICES

Physical Force
4-APPFS-3G-01
(Ref. 3-3175)

Physical force is used only in instances of justifiable self-defense, protection of others, and in accordance with appropriate statutory authority. Only reasonable and necessary force is employed.

Comment: None.

Protocols: Written policy and procedure.
Process Indicators: Agency records. Incident reports. Staff and offender interviews.

Incident Reporting
4-APPFS-3G-02
(Ref. 3-3176)

All incidents involving use of physical force are reported fully, promptly, and in writing to administrative staff for their information and review. All injuries are treated promptly and reported in writing.

Comment: None.

Protocols: Written policy and procedure. Report form.
Process Indicators: Agency records.

Transporting Offenders
4-APPFS-3G-03
(Ref. 3-3097)

When probation/parole officers transport offenders, the officers are equipped with authorized restraining and vehicle-safety equipment and are trained in transport procedures before being allowed to transport.

Comment: This includes agency-provided and personal vehicles.

Protocols: Written policy and procedure. Equipment inventory. Training curriculum.
Process Indicators: Staff records. Agency records. Training records.

Critical Incident Protocol
4-APPFS-3G-04
(Ref. 3-3098)

The agency has a process for immediate response, investigation, and further action and support in the event of a critical incident involving any employee.

Comment: The agency should determine its own definition for "critical incident."

Protocols: Written policy and procedure. Critical-incident-report form.
Process Indicators: Agency records. Documentation of response, investigation, and action.

PERFORMANCE-BASED STANDARD: VEHICLE SAFETY

3H. Agency vehicles are maintained and operated in a manner that prevents harm to the community, staff, and offenders.

Outcome Measures:
(1) Number of motor vehicle accidents resulting in property damage in the past 12 months divided by the total number of miles driven in the past 12 months
(2) Number of motor vehicle accidents resulting in injuries requiring medical treatment for any party in the past 12 months divided by the total number of miles driven in the past 12 months

EXPECTED PRACTICES

Annual Inspection
4-APPFS-3H-01
(New)

An annual safety inspection of all agency-owned or leased vehicles used in the field service operation of the agency is conducted in accordance with state laws, or by a qualified individual.

Comment: None.

Protocols: Written policy and procedure. Vehicle log format. Maintenance record format.
Process Indicators: Inspection reports. Completed vehicle logs. Maintenance records and receipts. Reports of vehicle problems/requests for repair or maintenance. Credentials of inspector.

Repairs
4-APPFS-3H-02
(New)

Safety repairs to agency vehicles are completed immediately. Agency vehicles are not used again until repairs are made.

Comment: None.

Protocols: Written policy and procedure. Maintenance record format.
Process Indicators: Maintenance records and receipts. Reports of vehicle problems/requests for repair or maintenance. Documentation that repairs were completed.

Insurance
4-APPFS-3H-03
(New)

Vehicles and drivers are insured in conformance with state laws.

Comment: None.

Protocols: Written policy and procedure. Copies of state laws.
Process Indicators: Proof of insurance.

OUTCOME MEASURES WORKSHEET

Standard	Outcome Measure	Numerator/Denominator	Value	Calculated O.M
1A	(1)	Number of offenders who are are arrested for any new criminal offense in the past 12 months		
	divided by	Total agency caseload in the past 12 months		
	(2)	Number of offenders who were convicted of any new criminal offense in the past 12 months		
	divided by	Total agency caseload in the past 12 months		
1B		None		
1C	(1)	Number of individual volunteers who provided services in the past 12 months		
	(2)	Total number of volunteer hours delivered in the past 12 months		
	(3)	Total number of hours of community service delivered by offenders in the past 12 months		
	(4)	Total number of hours of community service by offenders in the past 12 months		
	divided by	Total number of active offenders supervised in the past 12 months		
	(5)	Number of community entities (committees, boards, etc.) on which agency staff served in the past 12 months.		
	(6)	Number of presentations (speeches, panels, etc.) on provided to the community by agency staff in the past 12 months		
2A	(1)	Number of offenders who were discharged in the past 12 months		
	divided by	Number of offenders found in violation of a new criminal offense during the past 12 months (discharged and revoked)		
2B	(1)	Number of offenders found in violation of new criminal offense during the past 12 months		
	divided by	Total agency caseload in the past 12 months		
	(2)	Number of offenders found in violation of technical violation only in the past 12 months		

	divided by	Total agency caseload in the past 12 months		
	(3)	Number of offenders who absconded during the past 12 months		
	divided by	Number of offenders who were under active supervision in the past 12 months		
2C		None		
2D	(1)	Number of offenders who were employed on a specified day in the past 12 months (One day count)		
	divided by	Total agency active caseload on the specified day		
	(2)	Number of offenders who were employed upon discharge in the past 12 months		
	divided by	Number of offenders discharged in the past 12 months		
	(3)	Number of offender substance abuse tests for which the results were negative in the past 12 months		
	divided by	Number of tests administered in the past 12 months		
	(4)	Number of offenders who showed improvement as measured by the objective assessment instrument prior to discharge from supervision in the past 12 months		
	divided by	Total active offenders in the past 12 months		
	(5)	Number of offenders referred to drug treatment in the past 12 months		
	divided by	Number of offenders who successfully complete drug treatment in the past 12 months		
	(6)	Number of offender referred to education programs in the past 12 months		
	(7)	Number of offenders referred to behavioral programs in the past 12 months		
	divided by	Number of offenders successfully completing behavioral programs in the past 12 months		
2E	(1)	Number of offenders who had "stay away from" or "no contact with" or "no violence toward" orders during the past 12 months		
	divided by	Number of offenders who violated these orders in the past 12 months		

	(2)	Amount of restitution collected in the past 12 months		■
	(3)	Amount of restitution ordered in the past 12 months		■
	(4)	Number of offenders whose cases were closed with total restitution paid in the past 12 months		■
	divided by	Number of offenders whose cases were closed with restitution ordered in the past 12 months		
2F	(1)	Amount of court cost, fines, and fees collected in the past 12 months		■
	divided by	Number of offenders who had court cost, fine, and fee obligations in the past 12 months		■
	(2)	Number of offenders whose cases were closed with cost, fines, and fees ordered in the past 12 months		
	divided by	Number of offenders whose cases were closed with costs, fines and fees ordered in the past 12 months		■
	(3)	Total number of hours of community service performed by offenders in the past 12 months		
	divided by	Total number of offenders ordered to perform community service work in the past 12 month		■
	(4)	Total number of offenders who performed community service work in the past 12 months		
	divided by	Total number of active offenders supervised in the past 12 months		■
	(5)	Total number of offenders who participated in victim(s) awarness programs in the past 12 months		■
	divided by	Total number of active offenders supervised in the past 12 months		
2G	(1)	Number of offender grievances regarding discrimination filed in the past 12 months		■
	divided by	Total agency casload in the past 12 months		
	(2)	Number of offender grievances regarding discrimination resolved in favor of offenders in the past 12 months		■
	divided by	Total number of offender grievances filed regarding discrimination in the past 12 months		
	(3)	Number of other offender grievances filed in the past 12 months		■

	divided by	Total agency caseload in the past 12 months		
	(4)	Number of other offender grievances resolved in the favor of offenders in the past 12 months		■
	divided by	Total number of offender grievances filed in the past 12 months		
	(5)	Number of adverse judgements or consent decrees against the agency by offenders in the past 12 months		■
3A	(1)	Number of formal complaints against staff alleging improper conduct that were upheld or found valid in the past 12 months		■
	divided by	Number of formal complaints against staff that were filed in the past 12 months		
	(2)	Number of court decisions that found staff had acted improperly in the past 12 months		■
	(3)	Number of administrative decisions finding that staff acted inproperly in the past 12 months		■
	(4)	Number of hours of professional development attended by professional staff in the past 12 months		■
	divided by	Number of full-time equivalent professional staff positions in the past 12 months		
3B	(1)	Number of injuries to staff requiring medical treament in the past 12 months		■
	divided by	Total number of full-time equivalent staff in the past 12 months		
3C	(1)	Number of disciplinary actions against staff in the past 12 months		■
	divided by	Number of full-time equivalent staff positions in the past 12 months		
	(2)	Number of staff terminated for disciplinary violations in the past 12 month		■
	divided by	Number of full-time equivalent a staff positions in the past 12 months		
	(3)	Number of staff, contractor, intern, and volunteer substance abuse tests passed in the past 12 months		■
	divided by	Number of substance abuse tests administered in the past 12 months		

3D	(1)	Number of material audit findings by an independent financial auditor at the conclusion of the last audit		
	(2)	Number of objectives achieved in the past 12 months		■
	divided by	Number of objectives established for the past 12 months		■
3E	(1)	Number of grievances filed by staff against the agency or its representatives in the past 12 months		■
	divided by	Number of full-time equivalent staff positions in the past 12 months		
	(2)	Number of staff grievances decided in favor of staff in the past 12 months		■
	divided by	Total number of staff grievances filed in the past 12 months		■
	(3)	Total number of years of staff members' experience in the agency as of the end of the last calendar year		■
	divided by	Number of staff at the end of the last calendar year		
	(4)	Number of terminated or demoted in the past 12 months		■
	divided by	Number of full-time equivalent staff in the past 12 months		
	(5)	Number of staff who left employment for any reason in the past 12 months		■
	divided by	Number of full-time equivalent staff positions in the past 12 months		
3F	(1)	Number of fires that resulted in property damage in the past 12 months		■
	(2)	Dollar amount of property damage from fire in the past 12 months		
	(3)	Number of code violations cited in the past 12 months		■
3G	(1)	Number of grievances against staff alleging improper use of force upheld or found valid in the past 12 months		■
	divided by	Total agency caseload for the past 12 months		

	(2)	Number of grievances against staff alleging improper use of force filed in the past 12 months		■
	divided by	Number of grievances alleging improper use of force filed in the past 12 months		
	(3)	Number of court decisions against staff alleging improper use of force upheld or found valid in the past 12 months		■
	divided by	Total agency caseload for the past 12 months.		
	(4)	Number of court decisions that found staff had used improper force in the past 12 months		■
	divided by	Number of court decisions alleging improper use of force filed in the past 12 months		
	(5)	Number of administrative decisions finding that staff used improper force in the past 12 months		■
	divided by	Total agency caseload for the past 12 months		
	(6)	Number of injuries to offenders or others that required medical attention resulting from staff use of force in the past 12 months		■
	divided by	Total agency caseload for the past 12 months		
3H	(1)	Number of motor vehicle accidents resulting in property damage in the past 12 months		■
	divided by	Total number of miles driven in the past 12 months		
	(2)	Number of motor vehicle accidents resulting in the injuries requiring medical treatment for any party in the past 12 months		■
	divided by	Total number of miles driven in the past 12 months		

Definitions:

Active offenders: Offenders who are not on absconder status

Total agency caseload: Includes active offenders and absconders. "Total agency caseload" means beginning of the year active + beginning of the year absconders + offenders added during the year.

Revoked: Offenders who were sentenced to or returned to jail (misdemeanors) or prison (felonies) as a result of a technical violation or new conviction.

Discharged: Offenders who were removed from supervision for reasons other than revocation.

Appendix

Definition of "Qualified Individual" for Safety and Sanitation Inspections

Several standards refer to documentation and inspections by "qualified individuals." (For example, Building and Safety Codes (2A), Fire Safety (3B), Food Service (4C), Sanitation and Hygiene (4D), and Work and Correctional Industries (5A) standards.) Such persons also may be referred to as an "independent, qualified source," "qualified departmental staff member," "qualified designee," or "qualified fire and safety officer."

A "qualified individual" is a person whose training, education, and/or experience specifically qualifies him or her to do the job indicated in the standard.

I. General Requirements

When a standard calls for inspections, the individual conducting them needs to be trained in the application of appropriate codes and regulations. Standards do not specify the number of hours of training required, as this is determined in part by the tasks assigned. At a minimum, though, the qualified individual must (1) be familiar with the applicable codes and regulations and their requirements; (2) be able to use the appropriate instruments for measuring and documenting code compliance; (3) be able to complete checklists and prepare the necessary reports; and (4) have the authority to make corrections when deficiencies are found.

Training is often obtained from code officials or inspectors (fire marshals, building officials); government agencies that have statutory authority for inspections in a particular area (health department, labor department); or private organizations, such as the National Fire Protection Association. Often the individual obtains written certification or approval from these authorities to conduct in-house inspections. When trained and certified by the above sources to do so, a central office specialist may train and assist facility staff to conduct inspections.

II. Specific Requirements

A. Authority Having Jurisdiction

The term "authority having jurisdiction" is defined as follows:

The authority having jurisdiction must be knowledgeable about the requirements of the National Fire Protection Life Safety Code. The authority having jurisdiction may be a federal, state, local, or other regional department or individual, such as the fire chief, fire marshal, chief of a fire prevention bureau, labor department, health department, building official, electrical inspector, or others with statutory authority. The authority having jurisdiction may be employed by the department/agency, provided that he or she is not under the authority of the facility administrator and that the report generated is referred to higher authorities within the department/ agency independent of influence by the facility administrator or staff. This rule applies no matter who generates the report.

The definition also applies to the terms "independent, qualified source" and "independent, outside source."

B. Inspections

Qualified individuals conducting the monthly and weekly inspections required in the standards may be institutional staff members.

The qualified individual responsible for conducting monthly inspections (for example, fire and safety officer, safety/sanitation specialist) may be an institutional staff member trained in the application of jurisdictional codes and regulations. Periodically and as needed, this individual receives assistance from the independent authority or central office specialist(s) on requirements and inspections. This assistance may include participation in quarterly or biannual inspections. Training for the individual conducting the monthly inspections may be provided by the applicable agencies or through the agency's central office specialist(s).

The qualified departmental staff member who conducts weekly inspections of the facility may be an institutional staff member who has received training in and is familiar with the safety and sanitation requirements of the jurisdiction. At a minimum, on-the-job training from the facility's safety/sanitation specialist or the fire and safety officer regarding applicable regulations is expected, including use of checklists and methods of documentation.

The periodic weekly and monthly inspections may be conducted by either a combination of qualified individuals or one specialist, as long as the schedules and minimum qualifications described above are met. Safety and sanitation inspections may be conducted by the same person, provided this individual is familiar with the regulations for both types of inspections. When safety and sanitation requirements differ substantially, it may sometimes be necessary to call on several qualified individuals to conduct the inspections required by the standards. Using more than one person is strongly recommended.

III. Compliance Audits

In conducting standards compliance audits, the Commission Visiting Committees will review documentation submitted by the facilities to assist them in judging the qualifications of these individuals. In making compliance decisions, the audit teams will look closely at the facility's entire program—both practices and results—for ensuring safety and sanitation.

Glossary

Absconder – an offender who fails to report for probation or aftercare supervision; an escapee or runaway from a correctional facility.

Accreditation cycle – the three-year cycle between audits.

Accreditation manager – an agency employee designated to supervise the planning and implementation of accreditation activities in the agency. He/She has comprehensive knowledge of the agency and sufficient authority within the agency to design and administer a successful accreditation strategy.

Adjudicatory hearing – hearing to determine whether the allegations of a petition are supported by the evidence beyond a reasonable doubt or by the preponderance of the evidence.

Administrative segregation – separation from the general population administered by the classification committee or other authorized group when the continued presence of the inmate in the general population would pose a serious threat to life, property, self, staff, or other inmates or to the security or orderly running of the institution. Inmates pending investigation for trial on a criminal act or pending transfer also can be included. (See Protective custody and Segregation.)

Administrator - *See* Program director.

Administrator of field services – individual directly responsible for directing and controlling the operations of the adult probation and/or parole field services program. This person may be a division head in a large correctional agency, a chief probation officer answering to a judge, or the administrative officer of a court or parole authority with responsibility for the field services program.

Admission – process of entry into a program. During admission processing, the juvenile or adult offender receives an orientation to program goals, rules, and regulations. Assignment to living quarters and to appropriate staff also is completed at this time.

Adult community residential service – halfway house, community-based program providing group residence (such as a house, work release center, prerelease center) for probationers, parolees, residents in incarcerated status, and referrals through the courts or other agencies. Clients also may receive these services from the agency on a nonresidential basis.

Adult correctional institution – confinement facility, usually under state or federal auspices, that has custodial authority over adults sentenced to confinement for more than one year.

Adult local detention facility – local confinement facility with temporary custodial authority. Adults can be confined pending adjudication for 48 hours or more and usually for sentences of up to two years.

Affirmative action – a concept designed to ensure equal opportunity for all persons regardless of race, religion, age, sex, or ethnic origin. These equal opportunities include all personnel programming, such as selection, promotion, retention, rate of pay, demotion, transfer, layoff, and termination.

Aftercare – control, supervision, and care exercised over juveniles released from facilities through a stated release program.

Age of majority – the threshold of adulthood as it is conceptualized in law. It is the chronological moment when children legally assume majority control over their persons and their actions and decisions, thereby terminating the legal control and legal responsibilities of their parents over and for them.

Agency – unit of a governing authority that has direct responsibility for the operations of a corrections program, including the implementation of policy as set by the governing authority. For a community residential center, this would be the administrative headquarters of the facilities. A single community facility that is not a part of a formal consolidation of community facilities is considered to be an agency. In a public agency, this could be a probation department, welfare department, or similar agency. For a juvenile correctional organization, this would be the central office responsible for governing the juvenile correctional system for the jurisdiction.

Agency administrator – administrative officer appointed by the governing authority or designee who is responsible for all operations of the agency, such as the department of corrections or parole, and all related programs under his or her control.

Agency industries administrator – individual who has functional responsibility for industries operations throughout the correctional system. Titles, such as head of industries, superintendent, chief, director, or general manager, may be used for this position.

Alternative meal service – special foods provided to comply with the medical, religious, or security requirements. Alternative meals always must be designed to ensure that basic health needs are met and are provided in strict compliance with the policies signed by the chief executive officer, the chief medical officer, and for the religious diets, by the appropriate religious leader.

Appropriately trained and qualified individual for working with offenders with disabilities – one who has been designated by the warden, superintendent, or other authority, to coordinate efforts to comply with and carry out responsibilities defined by the Americans with Disabilities Act. That individual should develop relationships with, and use the expertise of institutional staff, advocacy groups, nonprofit organizations, agencies of government, and others that have relevant knowledge and experience.

Audit – examination of agency or facility records or accounts to check their accuracy. It is conducted by a person or persons not directly involved in the creation and maintenance of these records or accounts. An independent audit results in an opinion that either affirms or disaffirms the accuracy of records or accounts. An operational or internal audit usually results in a report to management that is not shared with those outside the agency.

Authority having jurisdiction – the organization or individual designated by statute, regulation, administrative rule or policy that is responsible for a specified activity, function, or operation within a correctional setting.

Booking – law enforcement process and detention-facility procedure. As a police administrative action, it is an official recording of an arrest and the identification of the person, place, time, arresting authority, and reason for the arrest. In a detention facility, it is a procedure for the admission of a person charged with or convicted of an offense, which includes searching, fingerprinting, photographing, medical screening, and collecting personal history data. Booking also includes the inventory and storage of the individual's personal property.

Boot camp – short-term correctional unit designed to combine elements of basic military training programs and appropriate correctional components.

Building code – *See* Code.

Camp – non-secure residential program located in a relatively remote area. The residents participate in a structured program that emphasizes outdoor work, including conservation and related activities. There are often 20 to 60 residents in these facilities.

Career development plan – the planned sequence of promotions within an agency that contains provision for (1) vertical movement throughout the entire range of a particular discipline, (2) horizontal movement encouraging lateral and promotional movement among disciplines, and (3) opportunity for all to compete for the position of head of the agency. Progression along these three dimensions can occur as long as the candidate has the ambition, ability, and required qualifications.

Case conference – conference between individuals working with the juvenile or adult offender to see that court-ordered services are being provided.

Case record – information concerning an offenders' criminal, personal, and medical history, behavior, and activities while in custody. The record typically includes commitment papers, court orders, detainers, personal property receipts, visitor lists, photographs, fingerprints, type of custody, disciplinary infractions, and action taken, grievance reports, work assignments, program participation, and miscellaneous correspondence.

Casework – the function of the caseworker, social worker, or other professional in providing social services, such as counseling, to individuals in custody.

Cases of exceptional merit – outstanding prison adjustment beyond that normally expected, performance of a meritorious deed by the inmate, or existence of an unusual employment opportunity for which the inmate is especially qualified and which would not be available at the time of the normal parole date.

Cellblock – group or cluster of single and/or multiple occupancy cells or detention rooms immediately adjacent and directly accessible to a day or activity room. In some facilities, the cellblock consists of a row of cells fronted by a dayroom of corridor-like proportions.

Chemical agent – active substance used to defer activities that might cause personal injury or property damage.

Chemical dependency – illness or disease characterized by physical and/or mental addiction to a mood-altering substance such as drugs, medications, and alcohol.

Chronic care – health care provided to patients over a long period of time; health care services provided to patients with long-term health conditions or illnesses. Care usually includes initial assessment, treatment, and periodic monitoring to evaluate the patient's condition.

Chronic illness – a disease process or condition that persists over an extended period of time. Chronic illnesses include diabetes, hypertension, asthma, HIV, seizures, and mental health disorders.

Classification – a process for determining the needs and requirements of those for whom confinement has been ordered and for assigning them to housing units and programs according to their needs and existing resources.

Clinical services – health care services administered to offenders in a clinic setting by persons qualified to practice in one of the health-care disciplines.

Clinicians – persons qualified to assess, evaluate, and treat patients according to the dictates of their professional practice act. These may include physicians, nurses, physician assistants, nurse practitioners, dentists, psychologists, psychiatrists, and social workers.

Co-ed correctional facility – institution designed to house both male and female offenders.

Code – any set of standards set forth and enforced by a local government agency for the protection of public safety, health, etc., as in the structural safety of buildings (building code), health requirements for plumbing, ventilation, etc. (sanitary or health code), and the specifications for fire escapes or exits (fire code).

Code of ethics – set of rules describing acceptable standards of conduct for all employees.

Commissary – an area or system where approved items are available for purchase by inmates.

Committing authority – agency or court responsible for placing a juvenile in a program.

Communicable disease – infectious condition transmitted directly or indirectly from person to person, animal/insect to person, or environment/object to person.

Community based program – see adult community residential service.

Community resources – human services agencies, service clubs, citizen interest groups, self-help groups, and individual citizen volunteers that offer services, facilities, or other functions that can meet the needs of the facility or have the potential to assist residents. These various resources, which may be public or private and national or local, may assist with material and financial support, guidance, counseling, and supportive services.

Continuity of care – health care provided on a continual basis beginning with the offender's initial contact with health care personnel and all subsequent health care encounters including referrals to community providers/facilities for offsite care during incarceration and when discharged from the institution.

Contact visiting – a program inside or outside the facility that permits offenders to visit with designated person(s). The area is free of obstacles or barriers that prohibit physical contact.

Contraband – any item possessed by confined juveniles or adult offenders or found within the facility that is illegal by law, or item used in a manner expressly prohibited by those legally charged with the administration and operation of the facility or program.

Contractor – person or organization that agrees to furnish materials or to perform services for the facility or jurisdiction at a specified price. Contractors operating in correctional facilities are subject to all applicable rules and regulations of the facility.

Contractual arrangement – agreement with a private party (such as an incorporated agency or individual) to provide services to juveniles or adult offenders for compensation. (See Independent operator.)

Control center – a very secure, self-contained unit designed to maintain the security of the facility. Policies governing the design, staffing, and accessibility of the control center ensure that it cannot be commandeered by unauthorized persons.

Controlled substance – any drug regulated by the Drug Enforcement Act.

Copayment – fee charged an offender by the correctional institution for health care or other services.

Corporal punishment – act of inflicting punishment directly on the body, causing pain or injury.

Correctional complex – more than one facility managed by the same jurisdiction located within close geographic proximity where services are shared or consolidated.

Correctional facility – facility used for the incarceration of individuals accused of or convicted of criminal activity. A correctional facility is managed by a single chief executive officer with broad authority for the operation of the facility. This authorization typically includes the final authority for decisions concerning the employment or termination of staff members, and the facility operation and programming within guidelines established by the parent agency or governing body. A correctional facility also must have a separate perimeter that precludes the regular commingling of the inmates with inmates from other facilities, a separate facility budget managed by a chief executive officer within guidelines established by the parent agency or governing authority, and staff that are permanently assigned to the facility.

Counseling – planned use of interpersonal relationships to promote social adjustment. Counseling programs provide opportunities to express feelings verbally with the goal of resolving the individual's problems. At least three types of counseling may be provided: individual (a one-to-one relationship), small-group counseling, and large-group counseling in a living unit.

County parole – status of a county jail inmate who, convicted of a misdemeanor and conditionally released from a confinement facility prior to the expiration of his or her sentence, has been placed under supervision in the community for a period of time.

Credentials – documentation that demonstrates health care professionals are qualified and currently licensed, certified, and/or registered, as applicable, to provide health services within their scope of practice.

Criminal record check – conducted in accordance with state and federal statutes to detect any criminal convictions of an individual.

Criminal – type offender - see delinquent youth.

Custody – level of restriction of inmate movement within a detention/correctional facility, usually divided into maximum, medium, and minimum risk levels.

Dayroom – space for activities that is situated immediately adjacent to the offender sleeping areas and separated from them by a wall.

dBA scale – a system for measuring the relative loudness of sound.

Delinquent act – act that, if committed by an adult, would be considered a crime.

Delinquent youth – juvenile delinquent or a criminal-type offender, a juvenile who has been charged with or adjudicated for conduct that would, under the law of the jurisdiction in which the offense was committed, be a crime if committed by an adult. (See also Status offender and Juvenile.)

Dental exam – examination by a licensed dentist that includes a dental history, exploration and charting of teeth, examination of the oral cavity, and x-rays.

Dental screen – system of structured inquiry and observation by a dentist, dental hygienist, dental assistant, qualified health care professional, or health trained personnel of newly arrived offenders to determine whether a dental referral or immediate medical attention is needed.

Detainee – person confined in a local detention facility not serving a sentence for a criminal offense.

Detainer – warrant placed against a person in a federal, state, or local correctional facility that notifies the holding authority of the intention of another jurisdiction to take custody of that individual when he or she is released.

Detention warrant – warrant that authorizes the arrest and temporary detention of a parolee pending preliminary revocation proceedings. A detention warrant should be distinguished from a warrant for the return of a parolee to prison, although return warrants are sometimes used as detainers. For the purpose of these standards, return warrants used as detainers also are deemed to be detention warrants.

Detoxification – treatment of a chemically or alcohol dependent person who is demonstrating symptoms of intoxication or withdrawal and/or the process of gradually withdrawing an individual from the substance on which he or she is dependent.

Developmental disabilities – a disorder in which there is a delay in the expected age-specific development stages. These disabilities originate prior to age 21, can be expected to continue indefinitely, and may constitute a substantial impairment in behavior and coping skills.

Direct care staff – any staff member who routinely has direct contact with the inmate population.

Direct supervision – method of inmate management that ensures continuing direct contact between inmates and staff by posting an officer(s) inside each housing unit. Officers in general housing units are not separated from inmates by a physical barrier. Officers provide frequent, nonscheduled observation of and personal interaction with inmates.

Director – *See* Agency industries administrator.

Direct threat – significant risk of substantial harm to the health or safety of any person including the applicant or employee with a disability which cannot be eliminated or reduced by reasonable accommodation.

Disability – physical or mental impairment that substantially limits one or more of the major life activities of an individual; a record of such an impairment; or being regarded as having such an impairment.

Disciplinary detention – a form of separation from the general population in which inmates committing serious violations of conduct regulations are confined by the disciplinary committee or other authorized group for short periods of time to individual cells separated from the general population. Placement in detention only may occur after a finding of a rule violation at an impartial hearing and when there is not an adequate alternative disposition to regulate the inmate's behavior. (See Protective custody and Segregation.)

Disciplinary hearing – non-judicial administrative procedure to determine if substantial evidence exists to find an inmate guilty of a rule violation.

Disciplinary report – a written report, prepared by a person with appropriate authority, describing an alleged violation of facility rules or regulations.

Dispositional hearing – hearing held subsequent to the adjudicatory hearing to determine what order of disposition (for example, probation, training school, or foster home) should be made concerning a juvenile adjudicated as delinquent.

Diversion – official halting or suspension, at any legally prescribed point after a recorded justice system entry, of formal criminal or juvenile justice proceedings against an alleged offender. The suspension of proceedings may be in conjunction with a referral of that person to a treatment or care program administered by a non-judicial agency or a private agency, or there may be no referral.

Due process safeguards – procedures that ensure just, equal, and lawful treatment of an individual involved in all stages of the juvenile or criminal justice system, such as a notice of allegations, impartial and objective fact finding, the right to counsel, a written record of proceedings, a statement of any disposition ordered with the reasons for it, and the right to confront accusers, call witnesses, and present evidence.

Ectoparasites – parasites that live on the outside of the host. Examples: fleas, lice.

Education program – program of formal academic education or a vocational training activity designed to improve employment capability.

Educational release – designated time when residents or inmates leave the program or institution to attend school in the community and return to custody after school hours.

Elective surgery – surgery that is not essential and is not required for survival; especially surgery to correct a condition that is not life-threatening.

Emergency – significant disruption of normal facility or agency procedure, policy, or activity caused by riot, escape, fire, natural disaster, employee action, or other serious incident.

Emergency care – care of an acute illness or unexpected health care need that cannot be deferred until the next scheduled sick call. Emergency care shall be provided to the resident population by the medical director, physician, or other staff, local ambulance services, and/or outside hospital emergency rooms. This care shall be expedited by following specific written procedures for medical emergencies described in the standards.

Emergency plans – written documents that address specific actions to be taken in an institutional emergency or catastrophe such as a fire, flood, riot or other major disruption.

Emergency power – an alternate power system that is activated when the primary source of electricity is interrupted. The system may be an emergency generator, battery-operated power pack or an alternate supply source.

Environmental health – conditions, circumstances, and surrounding influences that affect the health of individuals or groups in the area.

Expected practices – actions and activities that if implemented properly (according to protocols) will produce the desired outcome (achievement of the condition described in the standard).

Facility – place, institution, building (or part thereof), set of buildings, or area (whether or not enclosing a building or set of buildings) that is used for the lawful custody and/or treatment of individuals. It may be owned and/or operated by public or private agencies and includes the staff and services as well as the buildings and grounds.

Facility administrator – an official, regardless of local title (for example sheriff, chief of police, administrator, warden/superintendent) who has the ultimate responsibility for managing and operating the facility.

Field agency – unit of a governing authority that has direct responsibility for the provision of field supervision services and for the carrying out of policy as set by the governing authority.

Field services – services provided to delinquent juveniles, status offenders, or adult offenders in the community by probation, parole, or other agencies.

Field staff – professionals assigned case responsibility for control, supervision, and provision of program services to delinquent juveniles or adult offenders.

Firearm – a small arms weapon, such as a rifle or pistol, from which a projectile is fired by gunpowder.

Fire code – *See* Code.

First aid – care for a condition that requires immediate assistance from an individual trained in first aid care and the use of the facility's first aid kits.

Fiscal position control – process that ensures that individuals on the payroll are legally employed, positions are authorized in the budget, and funds are available.

Footcandle – a unit for measuring the intensity of illumination, defined as the amount of light thrown on a surface one foot away from the light source.

Formulary – list of prescription and nonprescription medications that have been approved by the health authority and are stocked or routinely procured for use in an institution.

Furlough – period of time during which a resident is allowed to leave the facility and go into the community unsupervised.

Good time – system established by law whereby a convicted offender is credited a set amount of time, which is subtracted from his or her sentence, for specified periods of time served in an acceptable manner.

Governing authority – the administrative department or division to which the agency reports; the policy-setting body. In private agencies, this may be an administrative headquarters, central unit, or the board of directors or trustees.

Grievance/Grievance process – circumstance or action considered to be unjust and grounds for complaint or resentment and/or a response to that circumstance in the form of a written complaint filed with the appropriate body.

Halfway house – *See* Adult community residential service.

Handicapped – having a mental or physical impairment or disadvantage that substantially limits an individual's ability to use programs or services.

Hardship cases – serious mental or terminal medical illness, imminent death, or death of a member of the inmate's immediate family.

Head of industries – *See* Agency industries administrator.

Health agency – organization that provides health care services to an institution or a system of institutions.

Health appraisal – a review of health care screenings and the collection of other health care data by a qualified health care professional that includes consultation with a health care practitioner.

Health authority – health administrator, or agency responsible for the provision of health care services at an institution or system of institutions; the responsible physician may be the health authority.

Health care – all action taken (preventative and therapeutic) to provide for the physical and mental well-being of a population. It includes medical and dental services, mental health services, nursing, personal hygiene, dietary services, and environmental conditions.

Health care personnel – individuals whose primary duty is to provide health services to inmates in keeping with their respective levels of health care training or experience as authorized by the governing jurisdiction rules and regulations.

Health care practitioner – health care practitioners are clinicians trained to diagnose and treat patients, such as physicians, dentists, psychologists, podiatrists, optometrists, nurse practitioners, and physician assistants.

Health care professional – staff who perform clinical duties, such as health care practitioners, nurses, social workers, emergency medical technicians in accordance with each health care professional's scope of training and applicable licensing, certification, and regulatory requirements.

Health care provider – individual licensed in the delivery of health care.

Health care services – system of preventative and therapeutic services that provide for the physical and mental well-being of a population. Includes medical and dental services, mental health services, nursing, pharmaceutical services, personal hygiene, dietary services, and environmental conditions.

Health code – *See* Code.

Health exam – a thorough examination of a patient's current physical condition and medical history conducted by or under the supervision of a licensed professional.

Health screen - a structured inquiry and observation to prevent newly arrived offenders who pose a health or safety threat to themselves or others from being admitted to the general population and to identify those who require immediate medical attention. The screen can be initiated at the time of admission by health care personnel or by a health-trained correctional officer.

Health trained personnel – correctional officers or other correctional personnel who may be trained and appropriately supervised to carry out specific duties with regard to the administration of health care.

Hearing – proceeding to determine a course of action, such as the placement of a juvenile or adult offender or to determine guilt or innocence in a disciplinary matter. Argument, witnesses, or evidence are heard by a judicial officer or administrative body in making the determination.

Hearing examiner – individual appointed by the parole authority who conducts hearings for the authority. His or her power of decision making may include, but not be limited to, making parole recommendations to granting, denying, or revoking parole.

Holding facility – temporary confinement facility, for which the custodial authority is usually less than 48 hours, where arrested persons are held pending release, adjudication, or transfer to another facility.

Holidays – days legally designated as non-work days by statute or by the chief governing authority of a jurisdiction.

House parent – *See* Program director.

Housing unit – a group or cluster of single and/or multiple occupancy cells or detention rooms that houses offenders and is immediately adjacent and directly accessible to a dayroom.

Improvement – *See* Quality assurance.

Incident report – a written document reporting a special event such as use of force, use of chemical agents, discharge of firearms, and so forth. The term is often used interchangeably with the term disciplinary report.

Independent audit – an audit that is completed independent of influence by the agency or organization being audited.

Independent operator – person or persons who contract with a correctional agency or other governmental agency to operate and manage a correctional program or facility.

Independent source – person, organization, or group that acts independently from the correctional unit being evaluated. An independent source may not be a staff member who reports to the chief executive officer of the unit being audited.

Indigent – individual with no funds or source of income.

Industries – activity existing in a correctional system that uses inmate labor to produce goods and/or services for sale. These goods and/or services are sold at prices calculated to recover all or a substantial portion of costs associated with their production and may include a margin of profit. Sale of the products and/or services is not limited to the institution where the industries activity is located.

Infection control program – program designed to investigate, prevent, and control the spread of infections and communicable disease.

Infirmary – health observation and care under the admission of a health care practitioner and supervision of a qualified health care professional; housed in a separate area from other general housing areas.

Information system – concepts, personnel, and supporting technology for the collection, organization, and delivery of information for administrative use. There are two such types of information: (1) standard information, consisting of the data required for operations control such as the daily count, payroll data in a personnel office, probation/parole success rates, referral sources, and caseload levels; (2) demand information, consisting of information that can be generated when a report is required, such as information on the number of residents in educational and training programs, duration of residence, or the number of residents eligible for discharge during a 12-month period by offense, sentence, and month of release.

Informed consent – informed agreement by a patient to a treatment, examination, or procedure after the patient receives the material facts regarding the nature, consequences, risks, and alternatives concerning the proposed treatment, examination, or procedure.

Inmate – individual, whether in pretrial, un-sentenced, or sentenced status, who is confined in a correctional facility.

Inmate compensation – incentives that are given for services provided. Incentives may be monetary compensation, special housing, extra privileges, good time credits and other items of value.

Institution industries manager – individual designated as responsible for industries operations at a specific institution in the correctional system.

Interstate compact on juveniles – an agreement authorizing the interstate supervision of juvenile delinquents. This can also include the cooperative institutionalization of special types of delinquent juveniles, such as psychotics and mentally disabled delinquents.

Interstate compact for the supervision of probationers and parolees – agreement entered into by eligible jurisdictions in the United States and its territories that provides the criteria for these jurisdictions to cooperate in working with probation and release.

Inter-system transfers – transfers from one distinct correctional system to another.

Intra-system transfers – transfers from facility to facility within a correctional system.

Jail – *See* Adult local detention facility.

Judicial review of Juveniles – a proceeding to reexamine the course of action or continued confinement of a juvenile in a secure detention facility. Arguments, witnesses, or evidence are not required as part of the review. Reviews may be conducted by a judge, judicial officer, or an administrator who has been delegated the authority to release juveniles from secure detention with the approval of the judge.

Juvenile – person under the age of 21 or as defined in the local jurisdiction as under the age of criminal majority.

Juvenile community residential program – program housed in a structure without security fences and security hardware or other major restraining construction typically associated with correctional facilities, such as a converted apartment building or a private home. They are not constructed as or intended to be detention facilities. Except for daycare programs, they provide 24-hour care, programs, and supervision to juveniles in residence. Their focus is on providing the juvenile with positive adult models and program activities that assist in resolving problems specific to this age group in an environment conducive to positive behavior in the community.

Juvenile correctional facility – an institution that may provide supervision, programs, and residential services for more than 100 residents. These facilities are designed and operated to be secure institutions. Juvenile development centers, juvenile treatment centers, secure training schools, and other facilities in the category may serve relatively smaller populations ranging from 40 to 100 juveniles. The age range served is generally from 13 to 18, although in many jurisdictions, residents may be as young as 10 or as old as 20. Older residents are usually juveniles who have been returned to the facility as parole violators.

Juvenile day treatment program – program that provides services to juveniles who live at home and report to the program on a daily basis. Juveniles in these programs require more attention than that provided by probation and aftercare services. Often the program operates its own education program through the local school district. The population usually is drawn from court commitments but may include juveniles enrolled as a preventive or diversionary measure. The program may operate as part of a residential program, and it may provide space for occasional overnight stays by program participants where circumstances warrant additional assistance.

Juvenile delinquent – *See* Delinquent youth.

Juvenile detention – temporary care of juvenile offenders and juveniles alleged to be delinquent who require secure custody in a physically restricting facility.

Juvenile development center – *See* Juvenile correctional facility.

Juvenile group home – non-secure residential program emphasizing family-style living in a homelike atmosphere. Program goals are similar to those for large community residential programs. Although group homes usually house juveniles who are court-committed, they also house abused or neglected juveniles who are placed by social agencies. Small group homes serve from four to eight juveniles; large group homes serve eight-to-12. Participating juveniles range in age from 10 to 17, with the concentration from 13 to 16.

Juvenile intake – process of determining whether the interests of the public or the juvenile require the filing of a petition with the juvenile court. Generally, an intake officer receives, reviews, and processes complaints, recommends detention or release, and provides services for juveniles and their families, including diversion and referral to other community agencies.

Juvenile non-residential program – a program that provides services to juveniles who live at home and report to the program on a daily basis. Juveniles in these programs require more attention than that provided by probation and aftercare services. Often the program operates its own education program through the local school district. The population of non-residential programs may be as many as 50 boys and girls ranging in age from 10 to 18. The population is usually drawn from court commitments but may include juveniles enrolled as a preventive or diversionary measure. The program may operate as part of a residential program, and it may provide space for occasional overnight stays by program participants where circumstances warrant additional assistance.

Juvenile ranch – non-secure residential program providing services to juveniles in a rural setting. Typically, the residents participate in a structured program of education, recreation, and facility maintenance, including responsibility for the physical plant, its equipment, and livestock. Often there are 20-to-60 juveniles in the ranch setting, ranging in age from 13-to-18.

Juvenile service center – *See* Juvenile correctional facility.

Juvenile village – *See* Juvenile correctional facility.

Library service – a service that provides reading materials for convenient use; circulation of reading materials; service to help provide users with library materials, educational and recreational audio/visual materials, or a combination of these services.

Life Safety Code – manual published and updated by the National Fire Protection Association specifying minimum standards for fire safety necessary in the public interest. Two chapters are devoted to correctional facilities.

Lockup – *See* Holding facility.

Mail inspection – examination of incoming and outgoing mail for contraband, cash, checks, and money orders.

Major equipment – equipment that is securely and permanently fastened to the building or any equipment with a current book value of $1,000 or more.

Major infraction – rule violation involving a grievous loss and requiring imposition of due process procedures. Major infractions include (1) violations that may result in disciplinary detention or administrative segregation; (2) violations for which punishment may tend to increase an inmate's sentence; (3) violations that may result in a forfeiture, such as loss of good-time or work time; and (4) violations that may be referred for criminal prosecution.

Mandatory standard – standards that have been determined by the American Correctional Association to directly affect the life, health, and safety of offenders and correctional personnel.

Management information system – *See* Information system.

Master index file – used in an institution to keep track of the inmates who are housed in particular housing units.

Medical records – separate records of medical examinations and diagnoses maintained by the responsible physician. The date and time of all medical examinations and copies of standing or direct medical orders from the physician to the facility staff should be transferred to the resident's record.

Medical restraints – chemical restraints, such as sedatives, or physical restraints, such as straitjackets, applied only for medical or psychiatric purposes. Metal handcuffs and leg shackles are not considered medical restraints.

Medical screen – *See* Health screen.

Medically trained personnel – *See* Health trained personnel.

Medication administration – process of giving a dose of a prescribed or over-the-counter medication to a patient.

Medication dispensing – the process of placing one or more doses of a medication into a container that is labeled to indicate the name of the patient, the contents of the container, and other necessary information by health care staff member as authorized by the jurisdiction.

Medication disposal – destruction or removal of medication from a facility after discontinuation of its use per local, state, and federal regulation.

Mental health care practitioner – staff who perform clinical duties for mentally ill patients, such as physicians, psychologists, nurses, and social workers in accordance with each health care professional's scope of training and applicable licensing, certification, and regulatory requirements.

Mental health screening – review by a qualified, mental health professional of any history of psychological problems and examination of any current psychological problems to determine, with reasonable assurances, that the individual poses no significant risk to himself/herself or others.

Mental health staff – individuals whose primary duty is to provide mental health services to inmates commensurate with their respective levels of education, experience, training, and credentials.

Mental illness – psychiatric illness or disease expressed primarily through abnormalities of thought, feeling, and behavior producing either distress and/or impaired function.

Mental retardation – developmental disability marked by lower-than-normal intelligence and impaired daily living skills.

Minor infraction – a violation of the facility's rules of conduct that does not require due process and can be resolved without the imposition of serious penalties. Minor infractions do not violate any state or federal statutes and may be resolved informally by reporting staff.

Mid-level practitioner – nurse practitioner or physician assistant licensed or credentialed to assume an expanded role in providing medical care under the supervision of a physician.

Natural light – the illumination from the sun; daylight.

NFPA – National Fire Protection Association, which publishes the *Life Safety Code*.

National uniform parole reports system – cooperative effort sponsored by the National Parole Institute that calls for the voluntary cooperation of all federal and state authorities having responsibility for felony offenders in developing some common terms to describe parolee (age, sex, and prior record) and some common definitions to describe parole performance. These types of data allow comparisons across states and other jurisdictions.

Non-applicable – term used in the accreditation process to describe a standard that does not apply to the correctional unit being audited. While the initial determination of applicability is made by American Correctional Association staff and/or the audit team, the final decision rests with the Commission on Accreditation.

Non-contact visiting – a program that restricts inmates from having physical contact with visitors. Physical barriers usually separate the offender from the visitors with screens and/or glass. Voice communications between the parties are typically accomplished with phones or speakers. Offenders that present a serious escape threat, are a threat to others, or require protection are often designated for non-contact visits.

Non-formulary medication – medications not listed in the approved institution or agency formulary.

Occupational exposure – exposure to potentially harmful chemical, physical, or biological agents that occur as a result of one's occupation.

Offender – individual convicted or adjudicated of a criminal offense.

Official personnel file – current and accurate record of the employee's job history, including all pertinent information relating to that history.

Operating unit – one distinct operation of the industry's activity, which may be operated as a cost center or separate accounting entity. It may take the form of a manufacturing operation (for example, furniture making or clothing production), an agricultural operation (for example, dairy or poultry farming, crop or orchard farming, cow or pig farming), or a service activity (for example, a warehouse, keypunch operation, microfilming process, laundering, auto repair, and so forth).

Orientation and reception – the reception period includes interviews, testing, and other admissions related activities; including distribution of information about programs, services, rules and regulations.

Out-client – individual who does not live at the facility but who may use facility services and programs.

Outcome measure – measurable events, occurrences, conditions, behaviors, or attitudes that demonstrate the extent to which a condition described has been achieved.

Parent – individual with whom a juvenile regularly lives and who is the biological, adoptive, or surrogate parent.

Parent agency – administrative department or division to whom the agency seeking accreditation reports; the policy-setting body.

Parole authority/Parole board/Parole commission – decision-making body that has responsibility to grant, deny, and/or revoke parole. The term "parole authority" includes all of these bodies.

Parole hearing – procedure conducted by a parole authority member and/or hearing examiner in which all pertinent aspects of an eligible inmate's case are reviewed to make a decision or recommendation that would change the inmate's legal status and/or degree of freedom.

Peer review – process of having patient care provided by a clinician reviewed and evaluated by a peer with similar credentials. An external peer review is completed by a medical professional not employed by the facility being reviewed.

Perimeter security – a system that controls ingress and egress to the interior of a facility or institution. The system may include electronic devices, walls, fences, patrols and/or towers.

Permanent status – personnel status that provides due process protection prior to dismissal.

Personal property – property that legally belongs to the offender.

Personnel policies manual – a manual that is available to each employee and contains the following: an affirmative action program, an equal opportunity program, a policy for selection, retention, and promotion of all personnel on the basis of merit and specified qualifications, a code of ethics, rules for probationary employment, a compensation and benefit plan, provisions of the Americans with Disabilities Act (ADA), sexual harassment and sexual misconduct policy, grievance and appeal procedures, infection control procedures and employees disciplinary procedures.

Petition – application for a court order or other judicial action. For example, a delinquency petition is an application for the court to act in the matter of a juvenile apprehended for a delinquent act.

Physical examination – evaluation of a patient's current physical condition and medical history conducted by or under the supervision of a licensed professional.

Placing authority – agency or body with the authority to order a juvenile into a specific dispositional placement. This may be the juvenile court, the probation department, or another duly constituted and authorized placement agency.

Policy – course or line of action adopted and pursued by an agency that guides and determines present and future decisions and actions. Policies indicate the general course or direction of an organization within which the activities of the personnel must operate. They are statements of guiding principles that should be followed in directing activities toward the attainment of objectives. Attainment may lead to compliance with standards and compliance with the overall goals of the agency or system.

Population center – geographical area containing at least 10,000 people, along with public safety services, professional services, employment and educational opportunities, and cultural/recreational opportunities.

Preliminary hearing – hearing to determine whether probable cause exists to support an allegation of parole violation pending a revocation hearing by the parole authority.

Pretrial release – procedure whereby an accused individual who had been taken into custody is allowed to be released before and during his or her trial.

Preventive maintenance – a system designed to enhance the longevity and or usefulness of buildings or equipment in accordance with a planned schedule.

Private agency – the contracting agency of the governing authority that has direct responsibility for the operation of a corrections program.

Probation – court-ordered disposition alternative through which a convicted adult offender or an adjudicated delinquent is placed under the control, supervision, and care of a probation field staff member.

Probationary period – a period of time designated to evaluate and test an employee to ascertain fitness for the job.

Procedure – detailed and sequential actions that must be executed to ensure that a policy is fully implemented. It is the method of performing an operation or a manner of proceeding on a course of action. It differs from a policy in that it directs action in a particular situation to perform a specific task within the guidelines of policy.

Process indicators – documentation and other evidence that can be examined periodically and continuously to determine practices are being properly implemented.

Professional association – collective body of individuals engaged in a particular profession or vocation.

Professional staff – social workers, probation officers, and other staff assigned to juvenile and adult offender cases. These individuals generally possess bachelor's degrees and advanced training in the social or behavioral sciences.

Program – plan or system through which a correctional agency works to meet its goals. This program may require a distinct physical setting, such as a correctional institution, community residential facility, group home, or foster home.

Program director – individual directly in charge of the program.

Prosthesis – functional or cosmetic artificial device that substitutes for a missing body part such as an arm, leg, eye, or tooth.

Protective custody – form of separation from the general population for inmates requesting or requiring protection from other inmates for reasons of health or safety. The inmate's status is reviewed periodically by the classification committee or other designated group. (See Administrative segregation and Disciplinary detention.)

Protocols – written instructions that guide implementation of expected practices, such as policies and procedures, training curriculum, offender handbooks, diagrams, and internal forms and logs.

Psychotropic medication – medication that exerts an effect on thought, mood, and/or behavior. Psychotropic medications are used to treat mental illness and a variety of disorders.

Public agency – the governing authority that has direct responsibility for the operation of a corrections program.

Qualified medical person – *See* Health care professional.

Qualified mental health person – *See* Mental health care practitioner.

Quality assurance – formal, internal monitoring program that uses standardized criteria to insure quality and consistency. The program identifies opportunities for improvement, develops improvement strategies, and monitors effectiveness.

Rated capacity – the original architectural design plus, or minus, capacity changes resulting from building additions, reductions, or revisions.

Reasonable accommodation – modifications or adjustments, which enable qualified applicants with disabilities to access the job application process or which enable qualified employees with disabilities to perform the essential functions of the job and to enjoy the same terms, conditions, and privileges of employment that are available to persons without disabilities.

Reasonably private environment – may vary, depending on individual and institutional circumstances, but is one which will maintain the dignity of the disabled individual in light of that person's disability

Records (juvenile and adult offenders) – information concerning the individual's delinquent or criminal, personal, and medical history and behavior and activities while in custody, including but not limited to commitment papers, court orders, detainers, personal property receipts, visitors' lists, photographs, fingerprints, type of custody, disciplinary infractions and actions taken, grievance reports, work assignments, program participation, and miscellaneous correspondence.

Referral – process by which a juvenile or adult offender is introduced to an agency or service that can provide the needed assistance.

Release on bail – release by a judicial officer of an accused individual who has been taken into custody on the accused's promise to appear in court as required for criminal proceedings.

Releasing authority – decision-making body and/or individual who has the authority to grant, deny, and revoke release from a juvenile institution or program of supervision. In some jurisdictions, it is called the parole board or the parole commission. (See Aftercare)

Renovation – significant structural or design change in the physical plant of a facility.

Responsible physician – individual licensed to practice medicine and provide health services to the inmate population of the facility and/or the physician at an institution with final responsibility for decisions related to medical judgments.

Restraints – devices used to restrict physical activity; such as handcuffs, leg irons, straight-jackets, belly chain.

Revocation hearing – hearing before the parole authority to determine whether revocation of parole should be made final.

Rule book, offender – a collection of the facility's rules of conduct and sanctions for violations defined in writing.

Safety equipment – primarily firefighting equipment, such as chemical extinguishers, hoses, nozzles, water supplies, alarm systems, sprinkler systems, portable breathing devices, gas masks, fans, first aid kits, stretchers, and emergency alarms.

Safety vestibule – grille cage that divides the inmate areas from the remainder of the institution. They must have two doors or gates, only one of which opens at a time, to permit entry to or exit from inmate areas in a safe and controlled manner.

Sally port – enclosure situated in the perimeter wall or fence of a correctional facility containing gates or doors at both ends, only one of which opens at a time, ensuring there will be no breach in the perimeter security of the institution. The sally port may handle either pedestrian or vehicular traffic.

School or home for boys and girls – *See* Juvenile correctional facility.

Secure institution – facility that is designed and operated to ensure that all entrances and exits are under the exclusive control of the facility's staff preventing an inmate/resident from leaving the facility unsupervised or without permission.

Security devices – locks, gates, doors, bars, fences, screens, ceilings, floors, walls, and barriers used to confine and control detained individuals. Also included are electronic monitoring equipment, security alarm systems, security lights, auxiliary power supplies, and other equipment used to maintain facility security.

Security perimeter – outer portions of a facility that provide for secure confinement of facility inmates/residents. The design of the perimeter may vary dependent on the security classification of the facility.

Segregation – confinement of an inmate to an individual cell separated from the general population. There are three forms of segregation: administrative segregation, disciplinary detention, and protective custody.

Segregation unit – a housing section that separates offenders who threaten the security or orderly management of the institution from the general population.

Self-insurance coverage – system designed to insure the payment of all legal claims for injury or damage incurred as a result of the actions of state officials, employees, or agents. In public agencies, the self-insurance program is usually authorized by the legislature. A "memorandum of insurance" or similar document is required that acts as a policy, setting the limits of liability for various categories of risk, including deductible limits. Approval of the policy by a cabinet-level official is also required.

Serious incident – situation in which injury serious enough to warrant medical attention occurs involving a resident, employee, or visitor on the grounds of the institution. A situation creating an imminent threat to the security of the institution and/or to the safety of residents, employees, or visitors on the grounds of the institution.

Severe mental disturbance – condition in which an individual is a danger to self or others or is incapable of attending to basic physiological needs.

Shelter facility – non-secure public or private facility designated to provide either temporary placement for alleged or adjudicated status offenders prior to the issuance of a disposition order or longer-term care under a juvenile court disposition order.

Special management inmates – individuals whose behavior presents a serious threat to the safety and security of the facility, staff, general inmate population, or themselves. Special handling and/or housing is required to regulate their behavior.

Special needs – mental and/or physical condition that requires accommodations or arrangements differing from those a general population offender or juvenile normally would receive. Offenders or juveniles with special needs may include, but are not limited to the emotionally disturbed, developmentally disabled, mentally ill, physically handicapped, chronically ill, the disabled or infirm, and the drug or alcohol addicted.

Standard – statement that defines a required or essential condition to be achieved and/or maintained.

Status offender – juvenile who has been charged with or adjudicated for conduct that under the law of the jurisdiction in which the offense was committed that would not be a crime if committed by an adult. (See also Delinquent youth.)

Strip search – examination of an inmate's/resident's naked body for weapons, contraband, and physical abnormalities. This also includes a thorough search of all of the individual's clothing while it is not being worn.

Superintendent – *See* Warden.

Temporary disability – a condition that can be treated with an expectation of full recovery. They are not the result of chronic conditions, are short term in nature and resolve over time.

Temporary leave – *See* Furlough.

Temporary release – period of time during which an inmate is allowed to leave the program or institution and go into the community unsupervised for various purposes consistent with the public interest.

Terms, conditions, privileges of employment – include, but are not limited to: recruitment, selection, and hiring; salary and compensation; benefits, holidays, leave, and work hours; promotion and advancement; staff development, including in-service training; and retirement, resignation, and termination

Therapeutic community – a designed social environment with programs for substance use disordered patients within a residential or day unit in which the social and group process is used with therapeutic intent.

Therapeutic diet – diet prescribed by a health care practitioner as part of the patient's medical treatment. Therapeutic diets can be ordered by physicians, physician's assistants, or nurse practitioners.

Training – an organized, planned, documented and evaluated or assessed activity designed to impart knowledge and skills to enhance job performance. Training is based on specific objectives, is job related, from an appropriate source, of sufficient duration, relevant to organizational need and delivered to appropriate staff.

Elements of Defendable Training:

1.   Based upon specific objectives.
        Performance objectives (intent of training)
        Formal lesson plans or functional equivalent (content of training)

2. <u>Must be job-related</u>
      Job analysis (new employee)
      Need resulting from problem analysis (existing employee)

3. <u>From an appropriate source</u>
      Qualified by credentials
      Qualified by knowledge and/or skills
      Qualified by performance
      "Delivery-Skills Qualified"

4. <u>Of sufficient duration (quantity of training)</u>
      Hours – how long did it take to learn?
      Must be reasonably related to the complexity/importance of the topic.

5. <u>Where something relevant is learned (quality of training)</u>
      Student feedback
      Student evaluation and proficiency testing
      Improved performance on the job
      Agency improvements

6. <u>Appropriate staff were attending</u>
      Topics related to job tasks and/or performance problems

Attendance documented with name roster and title/positions of staff that perform tasks or share problems

Training plan – a set of long- or short-range training activities that equip staff with the knowledge, skills, and attitudes that they need to accomplish the goals of the agency.

Training school – *See* Juvenile correctional facility.

Treatment plan – series of written statements that specify the particular course of therapy and the roles of medical and nonmedical personnel in carrying it out. A treatment plan is individualized, based on assessment of the individual patient's needs, and includes a statement of the short- and long-term goals and the methods by which the goals will be pursued. When clinically indicated, the treatment plan provides inmates with access to a range of supportive and rehabilitative services, such as individual or group counseling and/or self-help groups that the physician deems appropriate.

Triage – screening and classification of offender health care concerns by qualified medical staff to determine the priority of need and the appropriate level of intervention.

Undue hardship – an accommodation that would be unduly costly, extensive, or substantial.

Unencumbered space – usable space that is not encumbered by furnishings or fixtures. At least one dimension of the unencumbered space is no less than seven feet. In determining unencumbered space in the area, the total square footage is obtained and the square footage of fixtures and equipment is subtracted. All fixtures and equipment must be in operational position.

Unit management – Management system that subdivides an institution into units. The unit management system has several basic requirements:

1. Each unit holds a relatively small number of inmates. Ideally, there should be fewer than 150 but not more than 500 inmates.
2. Inmates are housed in the same unit for a major portion of their confinement.
3. Inmates assigned to a unit work in a close relationship with a multidisciplinary staff team who are regularly assigned to the unit and whose officers are located within the unit.
4. Staff members have decision-making authority for the institutional programming and living conditions for the inmates assigned to the unit within broad rules, policies, and guidelines established by the agency and/or the facility administrator.
5. Inmate assignments to a unit are based on the inmate's need for control, security, and programs offered.

Unit management increases contact between staff and inmates, fosters increased interpersonal relationships, and leads to more knowledgeable decision making as a direct result of staff dealing with a smaller, more permanent group. At the same time, the facility benefits from the economies inherent in centralized service facilities, such as utilities, food service, health care, educational systems, vocational programs, and recreational facilities.

Urine surveillance program – program whereby urine samples are collected on an irregular basis from offenders suspected of having a history of drug use to determine current or recent use.

Use of Force – refers to the right of an individual or authority to settle conflicts or prevent certain actions by applying measures to either dissuade another party from a particular course of action, or physically intervene to stop them. The use of force is governed by statute and is usually authorized in a progressive series of actions, referred to as a "use-of-force continuum."

Volunteer – individual who donates his or her time and effort to enhance the activities and programs of the agency. They are selected on the basis of their skills or personal qualities to provide services in recreation, counseling, education, religion, and so forth.

Warden – individual in charge of the institution; the chief executive or administrative officer. This position is sometimes referred to by other titles, but "warden" and "superintendent" are the most commonly used terms.

Work release – formal arrangement sanctioned by law whereby an inmate/resident is released into the community to maintain approved and regular employment.

Workers compensation – statewide system of benefits for employees who are disabled by job-related injury.

Work stoppage – a planned or spontaneous discontinuation of work. The stoppage may involve employees or inmates, acting separately or in concert by refusing to participate in institutional activities.

Youthful offender – person under the age of criminal majority in the jurisdiction in which he or she is confined.

Member of the Standards Committee
1976- 2010

A

Adams, Betty (TN) 1996-1999
Alarcon, Francisco (FL) 1997-2001
Albrecht, Thomas (DC) 1988-1990
Allen, Frederick R. (NY) 1982-1986, 1988-1990
Angelone, Ron (NV) 1986-1988, 1999-2004
Antoine, Janitta (LA) 1996-2000
Atchison, Jim (KY) 1976-1978
Aud, Kenneth J. (MI) 1994-1998

B

Bachmeier, Kathleen (ND) 2009-2013
Bailey, Paul E. (NV) 1980-1982
Beard, Jeffrey (PA) 2005-2011
Belleque, Lester E. (OR) 1982-1986
Bertrand, Roma (Canada) 1984-1986
Bittick, John Cary (GA) 2004 -2008
Black, James (CO) 1988-1990
Blake, Gary R. (GA) 1986-1988
Bogard, David (NY) 2002-2004
Borjeson, Terry (CT) 2000-2004
Braithwaite, John W. (Canada) 1976-1980
Branham, Lynn S. (IL) 1990-1992, 1994-1998
Breaux, Donald J. (LA) 1992-1994
Breed, Allen F. (DC) 1976-1982
Brown, Melvin, Jr. (TX) 1992-1998
Brown, Robert, Jr. (MI) 1988-1990
Brutsche, Robert L. (CA) 1988-1998
Budzinski, Ron (IL) 2006-2010

C

Campbell, Nancy M. (WA) 1986-1988
Carlson, Norman A. (DC) 1976-1978
Caruso, Patricia (MI) 2006-2008
Chamberlain, Norman F. (WA) 1980-1982
Clute, Penelope D. (NY) 1988-1990
Cocoros, John A. (TX) 1990-1992
Coleman, Ray (WA) 1986-1988
Collins, William C. (WA) 1984-1986
Corsentino, Dan L. (CO) 1996-1998
Coughlin, Thomas A. (NY) 1988-1994
Craig, Daniel (IA) 2006-2010
Crist, Roger W. (CO) 1982-1984

Crawford, Jacqueline (AZ) 1976-1992
Crosby, James V., Jr., (FL) 2001-2005
Cunningham, Su (TX) 1994-1996

D

Davis, Pamela Jo (FL) 1986-1990
Decell, Grady A. (SC) 1979-1982
Dennehy, Kathleen (MA) 2006-2008
Dismukes, Hugh C. (TX) 1980-1982
Dixon, Leonard (MI) 2002-2004
Dorsey, Helen Brown (WA) 1982-1984
Dorsey, Neil (NM) 1982-1984
Dunning, James (VA) 1994- 1996

E

Enomoto, J. J. (CA) 1979-1980
Estelle, W. J., Jr. (TX) 1976-1980
Evans, David C. (GA) 1988-1990

F

Farkas, Gerald M. (DC) 1978-1986
Farrier, Harold A. (IA) 1986-1992
Fitzgibbons, Mark (SC) 2001-2004
Fischer, Brian (NY) 2008-2012
Frawley, Michael F. (MO) 1996-2002, 2006-2008

G

Gagnon, John R. (WI) 1976-1980
Gamby, Jacqueline Jones (CO) 1980-1986
Garvey, Robert (MA) 2000-2004, 2006-2008
Gaudio, Anthony C. (VA) 1976-1978
Ghee, Margarette (OH) 1996-1998
Gibson, Steve (MT) 2006-2010
Giesen, Linda (IL) 1982-1984
Gispert, Ana (FL) 1982-1984
Glanz, Stanley (OK) 2008-2012
Goodall, Paula (OK) 1982-1984
Goord, Glenn S. (NY) 1996-1999, 2002-2006
Guillen, Rudy F. (VA) 1976-1982

H

Haasenritter, David K. (VA) 2008-2012
Hahn, Paul H. (OH) 1984-APPFS-1986

Hamden, Michael S. (NC) 1998-2002, 2004-2006
Hawk, Kathleen M. (DC) 1992-1998
Hegmann, Michael, M.D. (LA) 1998-2000
Hershberger, Gregory L. (KS) 1998-2002
Hill, Gary (NE) 1976-1980
Hill-Christian, Sheila (VA) 1996-1998
Hofacre, Rob (OH) 2006-2008
Holden, Tamara (OR) 1986-1988
Housewright, Vernon G. (IL) 1976-1982, 1984-1986
Humphrey-Barnett, Susan (AK) 1988-1992

I

Irving, James R. (IL) 1988-1994

J

Jackson, Ronald G. (TX) 1978-1980
Johnson, Perry M. (NH) 1984-1992
Jones, Justin W. (OK) 2008-2010
Jordan, James M. (IL) 1986-1988

K

Kehoe, Charles J. (VA) 1978-1982
Kelly, Marton (OH) 1976-1978
Kelly, Ralph (KY) 2000-2004
Kennedy, Robert (NY) 2006-2008
Keohane, Patrick (MO) 1998-2000

L

Lappin, Harley (DC) 2002-2010
Larivee, John (MA) 1997-2005
LeBlanc, James M. (LA) 2008-2011
Lehman, Joseph D. (ME) 1994-1996
Lejins, Peter P. (MD) 1976-1978
Linthicum, Lannette, M.D., CCHP-A (TX) 2002-2006, 2008-2010
Livers, Mary L. (OK) 1996-1997, 2008-2011
Livingston, Brad (TX) 2006-2013
Livingston, Shirley H. (FL) 1976-1979
Lucero, Penny (NM) 1997-2001

M

Manley, Harry A. (MD) 1990-1996
Martin, Bill (MI) 2000-2004
Maynard, Gary D. (OK) 1989-1992
McCartt, John M. (OH) 1976-1978
McCotter, O. L. (TX) 1984-1986
McGehee, R. Daniel (SC) 1998-2002
McMahon, John F. (NY) 1976-1978

Michael, Venetia T. (LA) 1998-2002
Milliken, William V. (UT) 1982-1984
Minor, John (MI) 1992-1994
Mitchell, Anabel P. (FL) 1984-1986
Moore, Margaret A. (PA) 1990-1996
Moore, Michael (FL) 2001-2005
Morton, Joann B. (SC) 1976-1980
Murray, Albert (GA) 2006
Myers, Victoria C. (MO) 1980-1994, 2005-2009

N

Natalucci-Persichetti, Geno (OH) 1994-2004
Nelson, Ray (CO) 1984-1986

O

Owens, George (OH) 2002-2004

P

Pappert, Ruth M. (IL) 1980-1982
Parrish, David (FL) 1992-1998
Patrick, Allen L. (OH) 1992-1994
Peters, Howard A. III (IL) 1992-1998
Petrovsky, Joseph (MO) 1982-1984
Phyfer, George M. (AL) 1976-1978
Pointer, Donald W. (MD) 1978-1980
Pugh, Julian U. (VA) 1978-1980

Q

Quinlan, Michael J. (DC) 1986-1990

R

Rapp, Marcella (CO) 1984-1986
Rees, John D. (LA) 1988-1992
Ridley-Turner, Evelyn (IN) 1999-2003
Rion, Sharon Johnson (TN) 1996-1997
Robinson, Carl (CT) 1982-1984
Robinson, Denise (OH) 2008-2010
Robinson, William B. (PA) 1980-1984
Robuck, Lucille (KY) 1976-1978
Rogan, Marilyn (NV) 2008-2010
Ross, Howard (TN) 2001-2005
Rosser, Paul (GA) 1984-1986
Rossi, Linda D'Amario (RI) 1980-1982
Ryan, Timothy (SC) 2004-2006

S

Scott, Wayne (TX) 1998-2002
Sexton, Ted (AL) 1998-2002
Sheridan, Francis (NY) 2002-2004

Shirley, Sue (TX) 1980-1982
Shope, John T. (NC) 1976-1978
Schmidt, Robert (DC) 1986-1988
Shumate, Denis (KS) 1990-1996
Simonet, John (CO) 1990-1996
Singletary, Harry (FL) 1988-1994
Sipos, Chiquita (CA) 1984-1986, 1992-1998
Smith, Paula (NC) 2009-2013
Stalder, Richard (LA) 1994-1996
Stickrath, Thomas J. (OH) 1997-2000
Sublett, Samuel J. (IL) 1976-1986, 1996-1997
Swanson, Virginia (WA) 1988-1990, 1992-1994, 1996-1998

T
Thomas, David (FL) 2002-2004
Thomas, Penny (TX) 1997-2001
Townsend, Cheryln (AZ) 2002-2004, 2006-2008

V
Vassar, B. Norris (VA) 1986-1988
Vigil, Celedonio (NM) 1990-1996

W
Ward, Frederick J. (NJ) 1976-1978
Washington, Odie (DC) 1998-2002
Weber, J. Robert (NC) 1982-1984
Webster, Marge (NH) 2008-2010
Weldon, Paul I. (SC) 1978-1980
White, William S. (IL) 1986-1988
Wilber, Harold (FL) 1998-2000, 2001-2004
Williams, Joe (NM) 2002-2004
Wilson, George W. (OH) 1988-1990
Wirkler, Norman E. (CO) 1988-1990, 1992-1998
Wrenshall, Allen F. (Canada) 1982-1984
Wright, Lester (NY) 2000-2002

Y
Young, Marjorie H. (GA) 1986-1988, 1990-1992
Youngken, Michael (KS) 1994-1998, 2000-2002

Members of the Commission on Accreditation for Corrections
1974-2010

A

Ackermann, John (NY) 1976-1977

Anderson, Elizabeth (DC) 2002-2004, 2008-2010

B

Black, James (CO) 1986-1988*

Blake, Gary (MD) 1979-1984

Bogard, David A. (NY) 2000-2004

Borjeson, Terry (CT) 1999-2000

Boswell, Anita (AL) 2002-2004

Braithwaite, John (Canada) 1980-1986

Branham, Lynn S. (IL) 1990-1998, 2000-2002, 2008-2010

Breaux, Donald J. (LA) 1990-1996

Brown, Mel (TX) 2000-2004

Brutsche, Robert L. (VA) 1986-1998

Budzinksi, Ron (IL) 2006-2010

Buss, Edwin G. (IN) 2008-2012

C

Campbell, Donal (TN) 1999-2000

Caruso, Patricia (MI) 2003-2004

Casselbury, Parkes (FL) 2002-2004

Catley, Dan (VA) 2000-2004

Charters, Paul (FL) 1979-1984

Chin, Arleen (NH) 2000-2002

Clarke, Harold (NE) 2000-2004

Clute, Penelope D. (NY) 1984-1990

Coate, Alfred B. (MT) 1975-1980

Cocoros, John (TX) 1988-1994

Coleman, Raymond J. (WA) 1984-1990

Corsentino, Dan L. (CO) 1996-1998

Crawford, Jacqueline (AZ) 1986-1992, 2002-2004

Crosby, James V. (FL) 2001-2005

Cunningham, Su (TX) 1992-1998

Curran, Patrick J., III (TN) 2008-2012

Cushwa, Patricia (MD) 2002-2004

D

David, Monica (FL) 2004-2008

Dennehy, Kathleen M. (MA) 2004-2006

DePrato, Debra, M.D., (LA) 2004-2008

Dietz, Christopher D. (NJ) 1980-1986

Dooley, Barbara (TN) 2000-2004

Donahue, J. David (KY) 2008-2010

Dunbar, Walter (NY) 1974-1975

Dunning, James (VA) 1990-1996

Dupree, James (AL) 1996-2002

E

Elias, Al (NJ) 1979-1980

Elrod, Richard J. (IL) 1984-1986

Enomoto, J. J. (CA) 1980-1986

Epps, Christopher (MS) 2004-2008

Evans, David C. (CA) 1988-1990

F

Fant, Fred D. (NJ) 1974-1978

Farkas, Gerald M. (PA) 1974-1978

Fitzgibbons, Mark (SC) 1996-2004

Frawley, Michael H. (MO) 1996-2002

Fryer, Gordon L. (IL) 1974-1978

G

Garvey, Robert (MA) 2000-2004

George, B. James, Jr. (NY) 1979-1984

Ghee, Margarette (OH) 1996-2004

Gladstone, William E. (FL) 1981-1986

Goodrich, Edna L. (WA) 1978-1982

Goord, Glenn (NY) 2002-2006

Green, Leslie R. (MN) 1979-1984

H

Haas, Scott (KY) 2008-2012

Hamden, Michael (NC) 1999-2004

Hamilton, William (OH) 2000-2004

Hammergren, Donald R. (MN) 1975-1979

Hattaway, George (TN) 1995-1996

Hays, Bonnie L. (OR) 1987-1992

Heard, John (TX) 1974-1978

Hearn, Pamela (LA) 2006-2010

Hegmann, M.D., Michael (LA) 1999-2000

Heyne, Robert P. (IN) 1974-1977

Hill, Janice (FL) 2006-2010

Hill-Christian, Sheila (VA) 1996-2004

Hofacre, Robert (OH) 2000-2004

Holcomb, Beth (VA) 2002-2006

Hopkins, Wayne (DC) 1974-1977

Huggins, M. Wayne (VA) 1983-1988*

I

Irving, James R. (IL) 1981-1986

J

Jackson, Ron (TX) 1990-1996
Jackson, Ronald W. (GA) 1992-1998
Jefferson, Ralph A. (WI) 1978-1983
Johnson, Perry M. (MI) 1986-1992
Jones, Justin W. (OK) 2008-2010
Jordan, James M. (IL) 1984-1996

K

Kehoe, Charles J. (VA) 1983-1988
Kennedy, Robert (NY) 2006-2010
Keohane, Patrick (MO) 1999-2000
Kinker, Jeannette (NM) 2000-2002, 2004-2008

L

Lamberti, Al (FL) 2008-2010
Lappin, Harley (DC) 2002-2006
Larivee, John (MA) 2001-2005
Lick, Alton (ND) 2003-2007
Liddell, Wayne (MI) 1996-2002
Linthicum, Lannette, M.D., CCHP-A (TX)
  2002-2010
Lucas, William (MI) 1978-1983

M

Maciekowich, Z. C. (AZ) 1974-1975
Mangogna, Thomas J. (MO) 1974-1979
Martinez, Orlando L. (CO) 1986-1992
Maue, Frederick (PA) 2000-2004
Mausser, Cynthia (OH) 2008-2012
Maynard, Gary D. (OK) 1990-1994, 2002-2004
McGehee, R. Daniel (SC) 1999-2002
McGough, John (WA) 1979-1984
McGowan, Patrick D. (MN) 1996-2000
McVey, Catherine (PA) 2006-2008
Minor, John (MI) 1988-1994
Moeller, H. G. (NC) 1974-1980
Moore, Edgar C. (Ted) (SC) 1982-1988*
Morrissey, Thomas H. (NC) 1979-1980
Murray, Albert (GA) 2004-2010
Myers, Kevin Bradley (TN) 2004-2010
Myers, Victoria C. (MO) 1982-1994

N

Natalucci-Persichetti, Geno (OH) 1996-2004
Nelsen, Anne M. (UT) 1999-2000

Newberger, Jay M. (SD) 1984-1990
Nichols, R. Raymond (NM) 1974-1976
Northrup, Madeline K. (OH) 2006-2010
Nuernberger, W. W. (NE) 1974-1979

O

Omodt, Don (MN) 1979-1980
Orlando, Frank A. (FL) 1986-1992
Owens, George III, CCO (OH) 2003-2007

P

Parsons, Michael (OK) 1994-1998
Patrick, Allen L. (OH) 1990-1996
Patterson, Wayne K. (CO) 1978-1983
Phyfer, George M. (AL) 1986-1998
Pinson, Michael D. (VA) 2006-2010
Pointer, W. Donald (MD) 1974-1977

Q

Quinn, Luke (MI) 1988-2000

R

Ramirez, Teresa V. (TX) 1994-2000
Rapp, Marcella C. (CO) 1977-1982
Reed, Amos E. (NC) 1976-1981
Riedman, Irvin M. (ND) 1975-1980
Rion, Sharon Johnson (TN) 2000-2004
Robinson, Denise M. (OH) 2008-2010
Rodriguez, Felix (NM) 1979-1980
Rogan, Marilyn (NV) 2008-2010
Ross, Howard R. (TN) 2001-2005
Rossi, Linda D'Amario (RI) 1981-1986
Rowan, Joseph R. (IL) 1974-1980
Rowland, Claudia (IL) 1999-2000
Ryan, Timothy (FL) 2004-2008

S

Scott, Thomas (FL) 1999-2002
Seidelman, Charles (KY) 2004-2008
Sexton, Ted (AL) 1999-2004
Sheridan, Francis (NY) 2002-2004
Shirley, Sue (TX) 1981-1986
Shumate, Denis (KS) 1999-2000, 2002-2004
Simonet, John (CO) 1990-1996
Singletary, Harry (FL) 1992-1998
Slater, Brad (UT) 2008-2012
Skeen, Barbara (SC) 2002-2004
Skoler, Daniel (DC) 1974-1979
Stalder, Richard (LA) 1994-2000

Stickrath, Thomas J. (OH) 1997-2000, 2008-2010
Swanson, Virginia (WA) 1984-1998

T
Thomas, David (FL) 2000-2004
Thompson, William (TX) 2008-2010
Townsend, Cheryln (AZ) 2000-2004
Tremont, J. Steven (LA) 1977-1982

V
Van DeKamp, John (CA) 1974-1976

W
Washington, Odie (DC) 1999-2002
Watson, Robert J. (OR) 1977-1982
Weber, J. Robert (KY) 1974-1981
Webster, Marge (NH) 1992-1998, 2002-2006,
  2008-2010
Wheeler, Martha E. (MI) 1974-1977
White, William S. (IL) 1983-1988
Wilber, Harold B. (FL) 2001-2004
Williams, Joe R. (NM) 2003-2010
Wilson, George W. (KY) 1982-1988*
Wirkler, Norman E. (CO) 1984-1990
Wright, Lester, M.D., MPH (NY) 2000-2006

Y
Young, Marjorie H. (GA) 1986-1998
Youngken, Michael (KS) 1994-2002

*Based on an extension of original term to corre-
spond with ACA election year.